The Revd Dr Cally Hammond is t
College, Cambridge. She began her
at Oxford and then at Cambridge, v
historians taught her the value of stories and ....
communicating truths and beliefs. This has stood her in good stead
for thinking about the Gospels and the early Church. As well as
working in academic life in Oxford and Cambridge, she spent seven
years in full-time ministry in rural parishes in the diocese of Ely.
She is the author of *Passionate Christianity: A journey to the cross*
(SPCK, 2007) and *Joyful Christianity: Finding Jesus in the world* (SPCK,
2009).

GLORIOUS CHRISTIANITY

*Walking by faith in
the life to come*

———— ◆ ————

Cally Hammond

SPCK

First published in Great Britain in 2012

Society for Promoting Christian Knowledge
36 Causton Street
London SW1P 4ST
www.spckpublishing.co.uk

British Library Cataloguing-in-Publication Data
A catalogue record for this book is available from the British Library

ISBN 978–0–281–06429–8
eBook ISBN 978–0–281–06700–8

Typeset by Graphicraft Ltd, Hong Kong
First printed in Great Britain by Ashford Colour Press
Subsequently digitally printed in Great Britain

Produced on paper from sustainable forests

For Huw Jones and Richard Howells,
dear friends, upstanding Welshmen,
and fellow servants of the servants of God

Contents

·

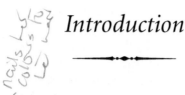

Introduction

John 21.25, RSV
There are also many other things which Jesus did; were every one of them to be written, I suppose that the world itself could not contain the books that would be written.

Hebrews 13.8, 20–21, RSV
Jesus Christ is the same yesterday and today and for ever . . .

Now may the God of peace who brought again from the dead our Lord Jesus, the great shepherd of the sheep, by the blood of the eternal covenant, equip you with everything good that you may do his will, working in you that which is pleasing in his sight, through Jesus Christ; to whom be glory for ever and ever. Amen.

What is a Christian?

I have been asking lots of people this question, and I've had an astonishing range of answers in reply. It could never be an easy question, because I insist that the answer has to be only one sentence long, so a lot of those who respond go away first and think hard about the matter before they give me their answer. It's not exactly scientific, I know, but that range of answers suggests that there is no consensus within grass-roots Christianity about what being a Christian really means. And at first that might seem to be rather worrying. If we don't know what Christians *are*, how can we know if we are being Christians in the right kind of way – whether that means doing it properly or doing it enough?

In fact I find this lack of consensus highly encouraging. It suggests that Christians are *not* people who define themselves by means of a check-list, either of 'correct' beliefs or of 'correct' behaviour. Some people have answered my question by referring to the Bible, or to the Church, or to their upbringing and education. Others start by rejecting a negative, telling me what a Christian is not – they point to their dislike of outsiders' prejudices about what a Christian is

('God-botherers', 'Jesus-freaks', 'Bible-bashers'). But the overwhelming majority of people who respond centre their reply on the person of Jesus himself. Very few people point first to the Trinity or the Scriptures. It is Jesus the man, the living human person, who has changed their lives when they first encountered him; and who continues to shape their beliefs, choices and lifestyle.

Christians are people who are convinced that there existed once a man called Jesus, who was known locally as Jesus son of Joseph (or, in his own language, Yeshua ben Yosef); that he was a teacher and healer in his own community; that he went to Jerusalem and got himself crucified by the Romans during the Jewish Passover festival. This took place in the days when the Emperor Tiberius Caesar ruled the known world (AD 14–37) and when a Roman called Pontius Pilate was governor over the quarrelsome province of Judaea (AD 26–36).

Christians are people who believe that this man Jesus was singled out by God. They refer to Jesus as God's 'Messiah' and 'Son'; these are titles which they have learned from their Bibles, or absorbed from the Church or from worship, or been taught by other Christians. A Christian is much more likely to focus on the question of Jesus' *true identity* than a non-Christian, who may be more interested in how Jesus behaved, and what he taught, than in the precise nature of his being.

Christians are people who believe that Jesus was a man (a real human person in historical time), but much, much more than that as well – because they have encountered him in their own lives. These encounters with Jesus take many forms, and are not usually based on the intellectual belief that Jesus rose from the dead and lives for ever at God's right hand. They are extremely difficult to put into words, or to explain. But they are powerful enough, and effective enough, to *make* people Christians and to *keep* people Christians.

So what is a Christian? If we turn to the Bible record of how it all began, we find that the first time the disciples of Jesus were given that special name was soon after his death: 'in Antioch the disciples were for the first time called Christians' (Acts 11.26, RSV). Those first followers were not called after his personal name, Jesus, but after his title or job description, 'Christ'. This means someone who has been specially marked with oil as a token of the task to which God has called him. The Greek word for one marked with oil in such a way is *christos*. In Hebrew it is *messiah*. These two words have come to be titles, 'Christ' and 'Messiah', and are so familiar that it is sometimes hard to keep in mind their true, original meaning. In particular we tend to think of 'Christ' as if it were Jesus' surname, rather than a description of his identity or his calling. Which is natural enough; after all, the system of calling people by a Christian name and a surname has developed in English in a similar way – many English surnames were originally job descriptions, or markers of function (Miller, Carter, Mason, Fletcher, Taylor, Cook, etc.).

When we think about calling Jesus 'anointed' or 'Christ', we have to get ourselves into the mindset of someone living in Bible times if we are to understand what the use of oil is supposed to be telling us. To use oil as a substance for marking things turns out to be highly significant. Oil leaves a stain which does not wash off, whether on fabric or on stone. To pour oil on something or someone is to mark them *indelibly* – the mark cannot be removed.[1] So to call yourself a 'Christian' means first that you recognize Jesus as God's anointed Son, and then that you yourself have been anointed – just as the oil leaves an indelible external mark, so the Holy Spirit leaves an indelible mark, though one which is not visible in ordinary sight. Because of this indelible mark, being a Christian means being different for ever, never being the same again. None of the challenges of life in the world around is different, none of the faults and habits of sin within you is different, but you have a new heart and a new spirit, and a calling and purpose in life.

If you are using this book for a post-Easter discussion or prayer group, perhaps you are thinking it's a bit late to start wondering *now* what a Christian is. But it is exactly now, in the immediate aftermath of the resurrection, that the friends and followers of the man Jesus began to see themselves as new, different, set apart, called and chosen. They began to explore a new way of relating to God, and to discover God's universal message of love for all the peoples of the world. They came to see themselves as the messengers (the Greek word for messengers is the same as the word for 'angels') of the good news of

---

[1] That is why anointing is still the most sacred part of the coronation of a new monarch – following the example of the Old Testament kings like Saul and David (1 Samuel 10.1; 16.13).

God's love. More than their loyalty, belief or support, more even than their racial origin, they were drawn together by their discipleship as followers of the man they recognized as Christ.

This, I think, is how God still wants us to see ourselves as Christians today. We are to be messengers of his love, his good news (which in the older English phrasing is termed 'gospel'). What's more, I think we have to try and see this with fresh eyes, to see past the clutter of old arguments – do you have to have a 'conversion experience' to be a real Christian? Do you need to be 'born again'? There is more than one way to discover that God calls us; and more than one way to proclaim his love for us. I think it is one of the unfortunate side effects of Christianity having emerged from Judaism (like a competitive younger brother or sister who needs to prove him- or herself) that Christians so easily spoke, and still speak, the language of oppression, victimization and persecution. It is an identity which fits that time of formation and self-defence against older ways well, but which in our time can encourage a siege mentality, of hostility to outsiders and suspicion of people who are not Christians.

In Bible times, the god(s) you worshipped depended on where you lived and what your racial origin was. If you were from Rome, your gods were Roman gods, who protected that city. If you came from Egypt, your gods had Egyptian names and were tied to that land and its people. If you were Jewish, your god (who had a name, but no one had spoken it for centuries, with the result that nowadays no one knows exactly how to say it any more) lived in the temple in Jerusalem and so that was where you went to make your offerings and seek divine help. This meant that in those days, for most people, religion was not something you could easily take with you wherever you went. One of the reasons the first Christians annoyed the Romans so much was that they claimed to be a proper religion, but did not follow the rules by behaving the way a proper religion would be expected to – they had no impressive temple or buildings; they did not practise blood sacrifice; they did not even have a racial identity – anyone, from anywhere, could become a Christian. It was radical democratic religion; and above all it was *portable* religion – it needed no special religious expertise. One of its most distinctive features was an enthusiasm for getting together in groups, for activities like singing and prayer. And in the Roman Empire that could spell trouble.

So the distinctive markers of the first Christians were these:

- a sense of shared loyalty to the man Jesus;
- a conviction that he was more than a man, and that he had overcome death;
- a belief that all who followed him would somehow participate in that conquest of death;
- a custom of meeting together for praise and worship both of God and of his Son the Messiah;
- the ability to carry their faith with them, and to spread the good news of Jesus and his victory wherever they went.

In a remarkably short time, these Christians had developed their own religious practices too, distinct from their Jewish origins. They had forms of worship which had an air of mystery about them, because non-believers were excluded (such as baptism and Holy Communion). *contrast* They also developed ethical principles which were meant to promote harmonious coexistence and to regulate their common life, many of which were based on Jewish teachings like the Ten Commandments. And they also built up a leadership system which was quite unlike anything the world had seen before. The Christian leaders at first were the twelve apostles; but as time went on successors had to be found, to carry on the apostles' work, and to oversee the well-being of the Christians. These leaders were called overseers and elders (the Greek words give us 'bishops' and 'presbyters'), and they strengthened the sense of purpose and direction among their flocks as well as keeping them true to the fundamental beliefs and teachings of Christianity. They were not chosen because of their noble ancestry or privileged rank, but through a common recognition of their calling, marked and authorized by the Holy Spirit. Such a leadership, based on quality and excellence rather than wealth or rank, was extremely radical for its time, allowing those with talent to come to the fore, regardless of their origins. This was bound to prove more successful than the alternative of being a religious authority merely because of your family background or political office.

Those first Christians were not marked out by their racial identity – you could not spot them by the colour of their skin, the language they spoke or the style of their clothing. They did not, in those very early days, wear crosses or other symbols openly to declare their religious allegiance to all the world. Yet they had no difficulty recognizing one another through their shared patterns of belief and behaviour. Above everything else they were distinctive for acclaiming the man Jesus as *more than a man* – as having a cosmic and eternal significance in God's plan; as being God's own Son; as having overcome death; and as having enabled his followers to share in the resurrection life.

This book explores what it means to be a Christian through the glorious mysteries, a traditional prayer which provides (instead of a set form of words) five fragments from Scripture for meditation:

- the resurrection
- the Ascension
- the coming of the Holy Spirit
- falling asleep
- crowning.

The five fragments, or glimpses, have been drawn together into one prayer, to complete the series begun with the joyful mysteries (focused on the Incarnation) and the sorrowful mysteries (focused on the crucifixion). For centuries this pattern of fragments has helped Christians to see how they are part of God's plan for humankind; to see how the life and death and resurrection of the man Jesus has meaning for them, in their time, in their life.

The first two glorious mysteries are extremely familiar from the Scriptures; they belong to Easter and its aftermath – the new beginning for God's people, the fulfilment of the promises. The last two have traditionally been associated with Mary the mother of Jesus, in the sense of seeing her as standing for us, for redeemed humankind, for everyone who has recognized Jesus for who he really is, and who has decided to live his or her life in the light of that new understanding. Between the mysteries focused on Jesus and those focused on redeemed humanity there is a pivotal mystery – and it faces in both directions, pointing back into human time and forward into divine eternity. Indeed, the giving of the Holy Spirit at Pentecost was for precisely that reason, to connect two apparent opposites, divinity and humanity, in an eternal bond, in a way that could never be broken – thus establishing a channel of communication which would never, and will never, fall silent.

Praying the glorious mysteries, more than the two meditations which precede it (the joyful and sorrowful mysteries, which I explored in my earlier books *Joyful Christianity* and *Passionate Christianity*) makes demands on our imagination which we cannot ever fulfil. It calls us to imagine heaven, our eternal and abiding home. It urges us to contemplate the miracle of miracles, from which Christianity was born – even though that miracle is never actually described in the whole of the New Testament! It also brings us into potential conflict (not for the first time in this series of meditations) with the world of science, and the realm of the 'probable'. This book is not about bridging the faith–science divide. It is much more about faith's journey in search of understanding. For God gave us our intelligence, and the means to use it wisely – the love of learning, of coming-to-understand, is of the very essence of our human nature.

Some Christians find the whole idea of resurrection a stumbling block. This is hardly surprising; the resurrection of a crucified criminal as God's anointed one was clearly a stumbling block in Bible days too (1 Corinthians 1.23). Such Christians may quietly omit that part of the Creed when worshippers declare 'I believe in the resurrection of the dead: and the life of the world to come'. This book is not meant to argue them into faith, or cajole them into saying what they find difficult or impossible. It is more an expression of faith as I understand it, and the reasons why I think that faith is reasonable, than an attempt to make everyone think exactly the same. So instead of making people feel that they can't be part of the Church any more because they don't believe in the right things, in the right way, we can find that it is possible, and acceptable to God, if we can simply manage to take some things on trust, rather than demanding nothing less than 100 per cent certainty. In the course of five chapters, taking each of the glorious mysteries in turn, I will make my way through some difficult terrain. I shall take as my guide the Scriptures, the wisdom of Christian tradition and the living faith of the present moment. Just as it is difficult to find a single answer to the question 'What is a Christian?', so it is also difficult to come to a single agreed reason for trusting in the message of Christian faith. In both cases we turn, for help, to the man Jesus, who was, and who is, so much more than just a man; and who shows us the way we must follow, the truth we need to guide us, and the life which will, in due time, be ours.

Of Heaven

O Beauteous God, uncircumscribed treasure
Of an eternal pleasure,
Thy Throne is seated far
Above the highest Star,
Where thou prepar'st a glorious place
Within the brightness of thy face
For every spirit
To inherit
That builds his hopes on thy merit,
And loves thee with a holy charity.
What ravish'd heart, Seraphick tongue or eyes,
Clear as the mornings rise,
Can speak, or think, or see
That bright eternity?
Where the great Kings transparent Throne,
Is of an intire Jaspar stone:
There the eye
O'th'Chrysolite,
And a sky
Of Diamonds, Rubies, Chrysoprase,
And above all, thy holy face
Makes an eternal Clarity,
When thou thy Jewels up dost binde: that day
Remember us, we pray,
That where the Beryl lyes
And the Crystal, 'bove the skyes,
There thou may'st appoint us place
Within the brightness of thy face;
And our Soul
In the Scrowl
Of life and blissfulness enrowl,
That we may praise thee to eternity.
Allelujah.

Jeremy Taylor (1613–67)

1

Resurrection

———•◦•———

Luke 23.50—24.11, RSV
Now there was a man named Joseph from the Jewish town of Arimathea. He was a member of the council, a good and righteous man, who had not consented to their purpose and deed, and he was looking for the kingdom of God. This man went to Pilate and asked for the body of Jesus. Then he took it down and wrapped it in a linen shroud, and laid him in a rock-hewn tomb, where no one had ever yet been laid. It was the day of Preparation, and the sabbath was beginning. The women who had come with him from Galilee followed, and saw the tomb, and how his body was laid; then they returned, and prepared spices and ointments. On the sabbath they rested according to the commandment.

But on the first day of the week, at early dawn, they went to the tomb, taking the spices which they had prepared. And they found the stone rolled away from the tomb, but when they went in they did not find the body. While they were perplexed about this, behold, two men stood by them in dazzling apparel; and as they were frightened and bowed their faces to the ground, the men said to them, 'Why do you seek the living among the dead? Remember how he told you, while he was still in Galilee, that the Son of man must be delivered into the hands of sinful men, and be crucified, and on the third day rise.' And they remembered his words, and returning from the tomb they told all this to the eleven and to all the rest. Now it was Mary Magdalene and Joanna and Mary the mother of James and the other women with them who told this to the apostles; but these words seemed to them an idle tale, and they did not believe them.

1 Corinthians 15.3–8, RSV
I delivered to you as of first importance what I also received, that Christ died for our sins in accordance with the scriptures, that he

1

was buried, that he was raised on the third day in accordance with the scriptures, and that he appeared to Cephas, then to the twelve. Then he appeared to more than five hundred brethren at one time, most of whom are still alive, though some have fallen asleep. Then he appeared to James, then to all the apostles. Last of all, as to one untimely born, he appeared also to me.

Human beings are afraid of the dark. Almost all of us are, for almost all of our lives. We associate light with hope and life, but darkness with evil and danger. So where does this primal fear come from? It could be psychological or genetic. It could be just plain common sense. At one extreme, fear of the dark has been explained as an instinct buried in our primitive evolutionary past, while at the other extreme, it has been dismissed as a behaviour which we merely learn from the way that other people behave around us. Yet any parent who has tried to settle a screaming toddler down for the night on his or her own in a dark bedroom knows that the fear is more than just about the dark itself – it is associated with being alone, cut off from sources of comfort, nurture and security. In other words, being separated from those who care for us and love us.

Darkness is where this chapter must begin, because darkness is the situation where the resurrection itself takes place, and so it is where the story of Christianity first unfolds. What is our attitude to darkness? It seems to me that fear of the dark is a natural instinct, not 'merely' a learned behaviour. Parents tend to hide their fears in front of their child, even when they are themselves very much afraid. They are usually more likely to react to their own fear by uttering some confident words of encouragement, an exhortation to bravery instead. A toddler, however, does not fear rationally (i.e. on the basis of an objective weighing up of potential or actual threats) but *instinctively*. For a small child, darkness means separation from visible sources of comfort and reassurance. It means an abandonment which, unlike the parent (who knows it to be both temporary and necessary) the toddler experiences as a danger, perhaps without end.

As adults, we can manage to rationalize this fear. Fear of the dark becomes fear of attack by strangers, the mugger, the rapist, the burglar. In exceptional circumstances, we may find ourselves alone and stranded, in the dark, away from civilization and the nearby hope of human help. That is when a very special kind of fear begins to assail us – in the ancient world of the Greeks and Romans it was associated with Pan, the god of woodland and the wild outdoors, and they knew it as *'panic fear'*, the fear which comes upon us suddenly, which is entirely beyond our control and can drive us against our will to do extraordinary things in response to the surges of terror. 'Panic flight,' says one expert, 'is the very antithesis of organized group behaviour' – it is highly individualistic, makes no attempt to deal with the perceived source of danger directly, and its principal physical manifestation is the act of running away.[1] Panic fear overcomes normal human control over impulses. In a time of panic, normal restraints on the desire to flee collapse, as does any concern about exposing oneself to laughter or criticism. So does the normal expectation of support and solidarity with others. Another writer notes:

> They used to teach that there is no fear of the dark; if there seems to be, the child must have been conditioned by some untoward event in a dark place – and as for the adult subject, such a thing is never mentioned, from which I can only conclude that writers of text-books have never been alone in the deep woods at night.[2]

If there is an apparently strong contrast between the world of the child and that of the adult, it may be not because adults have out-grown the childish emotion of fear, but because adults, in contrast to children, have developed a strong capacity for controlling their environment. By changing our habitual surroundings to protect our-selves, as adults we manage to minimize our experience of extreme situations; this means we are less likely to experience panic fear. On the other hand, we also become less aware of our susceptibility to it. In other words, we *think* that we are in control, and so feel safe, but in fact we have disguised our emotional vulnerability from ourselves. We have not eradicated it at all, we have just covered it up.

As well as thinking about our emotional and instinctive responses to darkness as negative and frightening, we also have to think about how we express those responses in words. We use the language of

---

[1] E.L. Quarantelli, 'The nature and conditions of panic', *American Journal of Sociology*, Vol. 60, No. 3 (1954), pp. 267–75; p. 270.

[2] D.O. Hebb, 'Review lecture: The evolution of mind', *Proceedings of the Royal Society of London. Series B, Biological Sciences*, Vol. 161, No. 984, pp. 376–83; p. 381.

light and dark in powerful ways, but often without much thought about the underlying reasons. This is not so relevant with babies and small children, but when we turn to how adults experience fear, our language is overwhelmingly positive about light and negative about darkness. We are aware of the seasonal shift between light and dark from summer to winter; we absorb into our positive and negative symbolism the fact that light makes things grow, while the change to decreasing light as midwinter draws near (i.e. the least light, the shortest day) makes plants shut down and stop growing. This is a simplification, I know, but with enough truth in it to help us understand how we 'feel' the language of light and dark. Conversely, it is the shift after midwinter to increasing light that kickstarts plants into active growth as they begin their cycle of reproduction once more, and the world wakes up to spring.

It is easy to see light as positive because light makes living things increase and grow. The harder question to address is whether the dark can also have a positive side. Can we uncover a theology of joy in darkness? Instead of seeing darkness as a season or a state which corresponds to what is negative (such as deprivation and barrenness), can we discover in it a positive side – embracing rest, and dormancy, and expectation? This is the question which the first glorious mystery, the resurrection, will inspire us to tackle.

But first, we have to come back to that opening question: is it 'natural' or 'normal' for human beings to be afraid of the dark? Some theorists believe that such fear is *learned* because our Western society associates night with what is unknown, irrational, wild and dangerous. It is not unreasonable that such fear of the dark is closely linked with a fear of being alone.[3] We are, in a sense, social animals – a fact which secular morality has lost sight of, but which is enshrined for ever in Christian thinking by the concept of the Church as the body of Christ. Not only do we need one another and depend on one another in practical terms, we also do so in psychological and emotional terms. To be alone is both an unnatural and a frightening state, and also – and this is the surprising part – something

---

[3] Harold Bloom (ed.), *Modern Critical Views: John Steinbeck* (New York: Chelsea House, 1987), p. 127; the first letter in the collection *A Life in Letters*, edited by his wife, Elaine Steinbeck, and Robert Wallsten (Harmondsworth: Penguin, 1976).

4

ct p16

necessary for the Christian person of prayer. The state of solitude, often accompanied by silence and darkness, is deliberately sought out as a strange and 'liminal' situation where extraordinary encounters with the divine may take place. 'Liminal' comes from the Latin word for a threshold, and it suggests a boundary between two worlds, two ways of being. Prayer is all about seeking out this liminal place, right on the boundary between safety and fear, and using it as a place of encounter with God, as we shall see.

In the Scriptures and language of Christianity, darkness is almost entirely negative. One New Testament letter tells us this on the authority of Jesus himself, saying that: 'This is the message we have heard from him and proclaim to you, that God is light and in him is no darkness at all' (1 John 1.5, RSV).

Right from the beginning, darkness is identified as a state of separation from God, while light is the first thing he creates after heaven and earth:

> The earth was without form and void, and darkness was upon the face
> of the deep; and the Spirit of God was moving over the face of the
> waters. And God said, 'Let there be light'; and there was light.
>
> (Genesis 1.2–3, RSV)

When Job endures his terrible sufferings, the worst curse he can think of is to curse the day of his birth as a day of darkness (Job 3.3–4), while his best hope is to depart from the pain of earthly life, by death, into a mode of existence where even the light itself is dark (an extraordinary paradox): 'To the land of gloom and deep darkness, the land of gloom and chaos, where light is as darkness' (Job 10.21–22, RSV).

The three books of the Bible which mention light the most are Job, Psalms and Isaiah. Of these, the Psalms mention light 22 times; Isaiah 23 times and Job a remarkable 29 times. For it is Job, more than any other Bible book, which wrestles with the question of good and evil, human suffering and divine justice. Light and dark are more than just symbols for Job, they are realizations, that is to say actual things rather than mere images or ideas, which *make real* what he must endure and what he nonetheless puts his hope in.

When we turn to the New Testament, we find a similar picture of light being associated with what is divine and holy. In Matthew's Gospel, Jesus tells his hearers in the Sermon on the Mount that *they* are the 'light of the world'. In John's Gospel, on the other hand, Jesus declares that he himself is 'the Light': 'I am the light of the world; he who follows me will not walk in darkness, but will have the light of life' (John 8.12, RSV).

This confirms what was revealed already by John as narrator:

> In him was life, and the life was the light of men. The light shines in the darkness, and the darkness has not overcome it . . . The true light that enlightens every man was coming into the world.
>
> (John 1.4–5, 9, RSV)

In these passages, there is the sharpest of possible contrasts between light and darkness, the light standing for goodness and divine truth while the dark stands for evil, concealment and lies. Paul follows the same line, albeit slightly less emphatically and fully, when he urges the Christians in Rome, whom he has not met, in that common language of light for good and dark for evil: 'The night is far gone, the day is at hand. Let us then cast off the works of darkness and put on the armour of light' (Romans 13.12, RSV).

His use of this language is exactly the same when he writes to Christians who came to faith through his preaching and teaching, and whom he knows personally: 'It is the God who said, "Let light shine out of darkness," who has shone in our hearts to give the light of the knowledge of the glory of God in the face of Christ' (2 Corinthians 4.6, RSV).

When Paul wants to challenge the Christians of Corinth to behave better, he phrases his warning in terms which equate light with righteousness and darkness with iniquity (2 Corinthians 6.14, RSV); there is a common pattern across his addresses to several different communities of believers, with light standing for openness and honesty, in contrast to deceit and concealment:

> Once you were darkness, but now you are light in the Lord; walk as children of light (for the fruit of light is found in all that is good and right and true), and try to learn what is pleasing to the Lord. Take no part in the unfruitful works of darkness, but instead expose them. For it is a shame even to speak of the things that they do in secret; but when anything is exposed by the light it becomes visible, for anything that becomes visible is light. Therefore it is said, 'Awake, O sleeper, and arise from the dead, and Christ shall give you light.'
>
> (Ephesians 5.8–14, RSV)

I have given quite a few examples of this language of light and darkness because it seems to me that the very familiarity of the light–dark contrast may be distracting us, so that we fail to notice how it is really being used, especially in the last few examples. For neither John nor Paul seems to think of darkness as a state which induces either reasonable fear or panic fear, nor do they treat it as a state which means physical danger for the one who enters it. Instead they see it as standing for corruption within the human individual, who prefers darkness to light as a way of concealing evildoing. If this understanding is correct, then here light must stand for the *absence of concealment* and therefore the impossibility of evil deeds: for that state of complete openness to God which is the aim of every Christian life.

So now we have two languages of light and dark to get to grips with. The picture is becoming more complicated than it seemed at first. We might assume that light is a simple fact of life, a reality which needs no explanation. But it is coming to stand for so much more: we soon find that being 'of the light' is a state we Christians must share with one another, and crucially it is a state in which we draw close to the image of God in which we were made. Again the examples from Scripture are too many to quote in full, but just a few examples make the point clear:

> You are all sons of light and sons of the day; we are not of the night or of darkness. (1 Thessalonians 5.5, RSV)

> The blessed and only Sovereign, the King of kings and Lord of lords . . . alone has immortality and dwells in unapproachable light, whom no man has ever seen or can see. (1 Timothy 6.15–16, RSV)

> You are a chosen race, a royal priesthood, a holy nation, God's own people, that you may declare the wonderful deeds of him who called you out of darkness into his marvellous light. (1 Peter 2.9, RSV)

This is driven home most emphatically of all in the words of John's first letter: 'Yet I am writing you a new commandment, which is true in him and in you, because the darkness is passing away and the true light is already shining' (1 John 2.8, RSV).

The culmination of this theme comes right at the end of the Bible, where God and his chosen people are finally united in the heavenly city:

The city has no need of sun or moon to shine upon it, for the glory of God is its light, and its lamp is the Lamb. By its light shall the nations walk; and the kings of the earth shall bring their glory into it, and its gates shall never be shut by day – and there shall be no night there.

(Revelation 21.23–25, RSV)

The ultimate conclusion of human history, when providence reaches its purposed end, is foreseen and recorded by the writer of Revelation, and this is the way we must take if we follow the glorious mysteries to their completion: 'Night shall be no more; they need no light of lamp or sun, for the Lord God will be their light, and they shall reign for ever and ever' (Revelation 22.5, RSV).

It could not be clearer, then, from the language of the New Testament that light belongs to the realm of the divine, and darkness to wrongdoing and rejection of the divine will and purpose. Despite traces elsewhere in Scripture that God reveals himself as the source of both light and darkness, good and evil (such as Isaiah 45.7), the prevailing view, especially in the New Testament, remains that darkness corresponds to secrecy and deceit, while light is the realm of openness and truth. But how does this question of light and dark in the Bible relate to the subject of this chapter?

In my previous two books in this series, I considered two principal beliefs of Christianity – the atonement and the Incarnation. It is here and now that we have to go backwards to where it all began: to the belief in which all Christian beliefs, even atonement and Incarnation, are rooted – namely, the resurrection. It is usually imagined as a scene of blazing glory – light bursting forth, as the stone is rolled away, or as the women encounter the angels when they come to honour the mortal remains of the man who had been Jesus. But it should not be. Not yet, anyway.

The mystery of the resurrection does not begin with the splendour of revelation but within the utter darkness of the sealed tomb: its stillness, its silence and its solitude. A man, the Son of Man, has died. His body is taken down from the cross. Time is short. The Sabbath, with its obligatory rest from all work, is looming. So his friends and followers hurry to put the man's body into a new-cut tomb. Then they roll a big stone over the entrance, and walk away as the Sabbath dawns. Now there are 24 hours to endure before the proper rituals of death can begin.

8

Every culture has its own rituals associated with death. The bodies of the dead may be washed and dressed in special clothes, or wrapped in a shroud or placed in a wooden casket. There are prayers to be said, songs to be sung, meals to be eaten, people to be contacted and summoned; priests to attend and rites to be gone through. The eyes must often be closed – not for the benefit of the dead person, but for the reassurance of the living. Eyes are the focal point of every human face. Open eyes mean contact and communication. Open eyes which convey nothing are profoundly disturbing to us, even distressing.

We make the dead person ready for the next stage of his or her journey, and we make ourselves ready for ongoing life in a world where that person no longer belongs. It goes without saying that this is always unsettling and can be dreadfully upsetting. The even surface of life's everyday fabric is rumpled and ripped, so that stitching it back together, smoothing it into its accustomed folds, can take a long time. Christians have become as distanced as everyone else in modern society from thinking clearly about the meaning of their own practices surrounding a death. On an emotional level, grief may be the most obvious factor to be accommodated, but it is by no means the only one. Deaths do strange things to us. Almost all of our rituals have the function of reassuring us that the dead person has really gone. If we are grieved by the death this may sound paradoxical, but I am sure it holds true. It is the fact of this terrible rending of life's fabric that makes it easy for us to delude ourselves about the meaning of the death, and in various different ways. We may spend years playing with the possibility that the person is not really dead at all, and will one day be on the doorstep ready to greet us when we get home. Some people experience regrets and guilt about their relationship with the dead person which are so traumatic that they fear the person coming back to haunt them in spirit form – to exact a penalty from beyond the grave for the breakdown in trust and love which happened long ago. This is more common in our society than one might expect, and most clergy have had to encounter such traumas and offer counselling and pastoral support in such circumstances from time to time.

If we look around us at those churches in our towns and villages which have grown up organically as part of the community, rather than being plonked or planted into them, one universal feature attests to the life–death divide with exceptional clarity: the churchyard. This is perhaps more obvious, because we can then see it with fresh eyes, if we compare it with other cultures. In ancient Rome, no dead bodies could be buried within the boundaries of the city – for that boundary formed a sacred barrier, one approved by, and protected by, the gods. The presence of the dead within it would be sacrilege. In this instance, we see the 'primitive' Romans having laws which enshrined their beliefs that the dead do not belong with the living, and that mingling of the two worlds was dangerous and contrary to the will of the gods.

This is not as different from our own behaviour as it might at first appear. If we think about our own communities, it is equally true of churchyards. We see the church rise up like an island in the midst of an encircling sea of the dead – a path picked out from churchyard gate to church door shows the safe respectable route into the sacred interior. Often the ground level is higher within the churchyard wall than outside it – perhaps a feature of natural geography, but equally likely the result of century after century of interment of bodies, and the heaping up of ancient bones.

How do people feel about churchyards? In daylight, they are nothing to cause concern. The nearest we come to that sense of liminality, that unspoken threshold or division between the sacred and the profane, is the sense of unease most people feel when treading on a grave. It evokes a feeling of discourtesy or disrespect – sometimes magnified by the mischievous imaginations of horror-film producers – and it remains, in my experience, something which most people instinctively avoid if at all possible. The Romans called the boundary between city-space and outer lands the *pomerium*, and held it sacred. So too the churchyard wall marks off sacred space – the land within it is set apart for divine use, and not for other purposes.

What of the churchyard at night? The graves have not moved, the trees do not rustle any more than in the day; but the churchyard at night can assume the proportions of a fearful thing in our imagination. I well remember how, when locking the church where I was rector, in the winter evenings I had to turn off the light and step out into what was (emphasized by the change from the light of the vestry) pitch darkness. My eyes soon grew accustomed; in time so did my mind to the contrast. But I never performed this simple action at night-time without the sense, dormant in the daylight hours, that I was stepping out of one world and into another.

Some people find graveyards disturbing places. This need not be, for a Christian has nothing to fear from the dead who are at rest. Any anxiety must come, then, from the nagging possibility that the dead are, after all, *not* at rest – that we must, as many other cultures do, propitiate them; or it could simply be a sense of the need to honour them, out of reverence or gratitude. This need not be driven by anything so monstrous or exaggerated as a fear of zombies or other terrors. It can be an entirely proper eagerness, in death as in life, to do our best for a loved one, to keep someone's memory bright by rituals of remembrance, whether religious (Easter, predominantly, in the Christian tradition, and All Souls), national (such as Remembrance Day) or personal (keeping birthdays and anniversaries). In Wales there persists a tradition associated with Palm Sunday (in Welsh it is called *Sul y Blodau*, which means Flower Sunday) of visiting the graves of dead loved ones and decorating them with flowers; it is memorably described in Susan Hill's book, *In the Springtime of the Year*.

One of the observable, practical functions of rituals, religious in origin or not, is to help people let go of their fears or anxieties. Where the dead are concerned, we have nothing to go on but our own sense that, in doing what we have done, we have somehow 'done enough'. The keeping of special seasons and days is particularly helpful in this regard, because it gives us a focus to which we can tie our need to remember, to connect. Otherwise, how are we ever to know if we have, indeed, fulfilled our obligations? It is rather like the old dilemma of certain extreme Christian sects about 'assurance of salvation' – how much prayer is enough? How much repentance will do for God? In the old days, there were guidelines (and the Church of England still offers them in her laws called the Canons) such as fasting on Fridays and in Lent, attending church and receiving Holy Communion at least at Easter and Christmas, and so on. Making a pattern of our observances is a way of giving ourselves a standard, so that we can be sure we have not fallen into neglect or abuse.

So the dead, by many means (some overtly religious, others not) have their ongoing place in our lives. There may well be an enduring undertone of anxiety about whether we have done enough and acted appropriately (this is probably true of every other form of human behaviour one cares to imagine too); and this is easily manipulated by those who want to sell us things – whether a slightly more expensive bouquet or coffin for the funeral, or a more gruesome horror film or console game. Whatever the emotions may be which are evoked by experiences of death, they are always powerful. Sometimes we accept this willingly, letting ourselves experience the fear in a controlled and limited way by watching a play or film, or reading a book, or playing a game. Thus we allow ourselves to undergo the feeling of being vulnerable without any real risk. But that is a completely different phenomenon from the real experience of fear, of suffering and death neither wished for nor co-operated in, such as people endure in bereavement, trauma, sickness or war. That kind of fear, those powerful emotions, scar the soul for ever.

We need to keep that distinction clear, between an experience of what (for want of a better term) we may call 'human darkness' as something willingly entered into for entertainment or the widening of our horizons, and 'human darkness' of the kind which is inescapably endured. When we, as Christians, approach the subject of the resurrection of Jesus, we may do it to be involved in the story (by watching a film); to broaden our emotional horizons (through reading novels, e.g. *Christ Recrucified* or *The Last Temptation* by Nikos Kazantzakis); by 'realizing' the gospel story (through participating in a passion play or an act of worship); by deepening our spiritual awareness (through reading Scripture); or even – most fundamentally – coming to fresh understanding of the nature of that event (through prayer). But we must admit that none of these experiences, however profound, however realistic, is ever *real* in the way that the actual resurrection of the man Jesus, in Palestine, in historical time, was *real*. Our approaches towards that reality may give us insight into the meaning of the event itself, or its personal significance for ourselves, or the hope it offers to others: but all of them, even worship and prayer, are still essentially different from the original event itself. This is because we cannot be more than spectators, or, at the most, participants, in the drama of what is unfolding. Even if we manage to achieve a sense of what it is to be a participant we are still, always, subsidiary characters, never the main protagonist.

Where does all this leave us as we attempt what begins to seem completely impossible? If we cannot even imagine the resurrection, never mind understand it, how can we become part of it? What can it possibly mean for us? How on earth are we to *pray* it?

Some of the details in the Gospel accounts of the passion and death of Jesus are so simple and practical that they put paid to any possibility of our modifying the story to make it less blunt and more 'spiritual'. It is a key tenet of belief in the resurrection of Jesus that when he was taken down from the cross he was really and truly dead. He was not in a coma or suspended state of being, but dead. As such, he no longer belongs in the world of the living, the world of light. His body is hastily wrapped up and put away. Why is a stone rolled over the entrance? For several interconnected reasons. The story of Lazarus reminds us that beyond our range of vision, buried in the earth or hidden in the tomb, dead bodies decay – in that case the dead man's sister is worried that there will be a smell of putrefaction (John 11.39). So the bodies of the dead are sealed up: to prevent the smell of decay seeping out, or scavenging animals getting in, but also to prevent living people encountering the dead body. The Jewish law was very clear on the point that physical contact with a dead body puts us in a different state of being. 'He who touches the dead body of any person shall be unclean seven days' (Numbers 19.11, rsv). This is nothing to do with the transmission of infection or disease. It is rather about the recognition that in touching a dead body, or even being in the presence of one, living human beings are encountering a different world, are standing on the threshold between one form of being and another – and this encounter is so powerful that it needs the reassurance of customary actions and rituals to restore normality. Such things can help us through the transition back to where we really belong, as living beings, in the light.

What about the dead body of the crucified man Jesus? No one knows what happened inside the tomb, or when. At some point between the rolling of the stone across the door, when the women ended their lamenting and departed and the guard was posted, and the arrival of the women on the third day to do proper honour to the mortal remains of the man Jesus, something unknown, and entirely 'other', happened. In ordinary Christian living, there is extraordinarily little writing, teaching, discussion or preaching which attempts the feat of imagining what went on inside the tomb. There was, of course, speculation in the early days of the new faith. One writer of an early Christian text called the 'Gospel of Peter' (because the writer claims that identity for himself) tried to supply some of the appropriate details which he felt were lacking in the four canonical Gospels:

> During the night, when the Lord's day was dawning, and while soldiers were keeping guard in pairs, there was a great voice in the heaven, and they saw the heavens opened, and two men coming down from there having much glory and halting at the tomb. That stone which had been rolled against the door now began to roll away from it by itself and made way in turn, and the tomb opened and both the young men went in. Those soldiers saw this and woke the centurion and the elders (for they too were there standing guard), and while they were describing what they saw they now observed three men emerging from the tomb, the two supporting the other, and a cross following them, and the heads of the two reaching to the heaven, and of the one being led above them, towering above the heavens, and they heard a voice from the heavens saying, 'Have you proclaimed to those who sleep?' And the answer was heard from the cross – 'Yes'.[4]

This late account 'smells of the lamp', as the old saying has it. It does not come across as a genuine eye-witness account. There is far too much emphasis on corroborating the facts of what happened, on the spectacle and miracle, and far too much is made of the symbolism of the cross (which in reality took the first Christians decades to come to terms with and understand).

The real Gospels make no such dodgy efforts to fill in the gaps. They are content to leave us with questions and mysteries. They do not try to account for those dark hours, in which the dead body of the man Jesus was hidden from human sight in the tomb. They do not suggest that during that time Jesus was descending to the realm of the dead to proclaim the good news to them, so that the grace of God could be extended to everyone who has ever lived. That is a belief which belonged to a later stage of understanding, not to the first generation in which the resurrection was expressed.

So if we follow the true primary witness of the Gospels, the resurrection is left mysterious. It is most certainly not explained away.

---

[4] My translation, from the edition of M.G. Mara, *Evangile de Pierre* (Paris: Editions du Cerf, 1973), pp. 35–42.

Instead it remains the shrouded, beating heart of our faith – for inside that place of darkness, imprisonment and decay, something happened which was for them, as it is for us, contrary to every known law of nature and life. Not the reanimation of a corpse, but the emergence of a new form of life never yet encountered in all creation. This is the first mystery for us to explore in our journey into the heart of our faith. It takes us to places of darkness, where we might expect to encounter fear and horror; but instead we find all things, ultimately, transformed into light and glory. In the end even darkness itself will be redeemed and renewed. It is as if the tomb of the grave were turned into the womb of new birth – where darkness no longer means danger, evil and death, but now nurture, protection and ultimately unification with the very essence of divine love.

This is all very well; but why does it matter to us, today? We have so little information, and (after all these centuries have passed) no means of getting any closer to the truth of those stupendous events. So what makes us keep asking, wondering, imagining? And what value is there in this present exploration? The clue is in the second of the two readings at the start of this chapter: a precious fragment of Paul's own past, as he relates to us what he himself was taught when he embraced the new faith:

> Christ died for our sins in accordance with the scriptures . . . he was buried . . . he was raised on the third day in accordance with the scriptures, and . . . he appeared to Cephas, then to the twelve.

What Paul learned, and what he spent the rest of his life preaching, was that the death of Christ was a fulfilment of Old Testament prophecy, and that likewise his *raising on the third day* was something which the Old Testament Scripture had foretold. So he insists that the miracle of miracles, the resurrection (which is unwitnessed, and ultimately mysterious to us) was part of God's plan for humankind, and that as such it had been foretold in his holy word. This 'in accordance with the scriptures' is repeated to emphasize that Paul's message, his good news, is not his own invention but a gift from God, to him, and in our day to us also.

Yet the dark enigma still remains at the centre, as impossible to imagine as the problem of suffering is impossible to answer. What happened in the darkness of the closed tomb of Jesus?

Whenever we celebrate something in our everyday lives, we do so because it has a meaning for us. Every time we repeat that celebration, the event takes on an added layer of meaning, varnished with the memories and associations of people and places which matter to us. We celebrate the resurrection every year at Easter; and we are meant to mark it with rejoicing every Sunday, because Sunday became the new Sabbath for those first Christians – the Jewish Sabbath made way for the Christian Lord's Day. There is a real question here about how good we are at making this so in our lives as Christian individuals and in our communities as Christian churches. Perhaps this has something to do with the fact that we don't really understand – nobody properly explains to us – that we are the resurrection people. That fact is believed in but unwitnessed; it is a living certainty though its process and event are quite inexplicable. It ought to be the hallmark of our faith. It used to be so in centuries past. One of the chief attractions of Christianity in the first centuries of its history was that it gave a sure promise that death was not to be the end of us; that we would, somehow, participate in the resurrection of which Jesus, now Jesus *Christ*, is the first-fruits.

So we are drawn to belief in a historical *something* of which we have no direct knowledge, but which we can draw firm conclusions about because of our human, God-given, ability to *reason*. As Sherlock Holmes would do, we look at the known facts (the empty tomb, the stone rolled away, the appearance of angels with their message for humankind, the appearances of Jesus to those who knew him), we exclude whatever can be excluded (he didn't really die, someone stole the body, etc.) and arrive at the only explanation which is left, namely that truth which God has made known in advance to us through sacred writings.

There is no proof of the resurrection, there is no explanation: it took years and years to work out the full implications. At this early stage, when Paul is writing, we can see no further than his remarks here allow us. But they let us in a long way.

The darkness within the tomb must have been absolute. No chinks of light, of that stuff which we associate with hope. Yet it is in this stillness, silence and solitude of pure darkness that the truth of divine love breaks out into human history. This is the same state that a Christian tries to recreate in meditative prayer. By excluding all that distracts us, we can find that inner stillness, silence and solitude for ourselves, and in it seek after God, and perhaps even encounter him directly.

Why do we believe in the resurrection of Jesus Christ? And why do we link it with belief in our own resurrection after death? Partly because of the witness of our sacred writings, but not entirely so. We are also always taking the person of Jesus the man into account. We are always looking at how he behaved and what he proclaimed in life: and there is no doubt whatever that for the man Jesus there would be a life after this life, in which we will remain recognizably the person we now are in our earthly life.

Belief in the resurrection comes to us as a gift from God, a gift we may wish to explore and examine, or to accept and rejoice in, or both. It should never be something we take for granted. If we have the courage to try to reflect, to meditate, on what happened inside the darkness of the tomb that night, we have found one way to keep over-familiarity at bay – the miracle of miracles, by its very mysteriousness, stops us from thinking of it ever as part of 'ordinary' life.

Fear of the dark comes to be something which in adult life we associate with our childhood, and which we believe we have outgrown as mature people. But it never really leaves us. After all, we are so much more than our thinking, rational self-consciousness. We are instinctive, genetic, hormonal bundles of motivation and instinct which we cannot understand or explain. Our hearts react to the story of the empty tomb, the witness of the women and the reactions of the men; and to the effect of its incredible good news of divine love. Somehow, in a deep unreasoned way, it chimes a melody of hidden truth within us: that it is not arrogant or deluded to believe that we matter to God as the people that we are; that the event itself holds a message for us all, of good news.

The tomb of the dead Jesus is a place of darkness and hope together. It is a symbol of how the familiar categories of our thinking are about to be overturned. For it turns out that darkness is not, in this case, a state in which decay and corruption hold sway; nor is it the setting for the dissolution of a unique person into the earth from which we all come, dust to dust (Genesis 3.19). Instead it is a threshold between one way of being (ordinary human life in the world) and another (eternal life, for which God destined human beings) which all of us will one day cross. Jesus is the firstborn in this new creation, showing the way and offering that hope for which we yearn that death is not the end of us, but only the end of our beginning.

The darkness and the light to God are both alike, for he created both (Psalm 139.12). The darkness is transformed by the resurrection into something we no longer fear as do little children. Instead, it has now become a liminal place where we must go to seek God out. Why it should be that darkness is a powerful state for prayer I do not know, but for myself I have found it to be true. One of the Scriptures which speaks to me most strongly of the tomb, the holy sepulchre, the burial place of Christ, is a verse from Psalm 32: 'Thou art a place to hide me in, thou shalt preserve me from trouble: thou shalt compass me about with songs of deliverance' (v. 7; Miles Coverdale's translation, BCP 1662).

God is our refuge and hiding place: a place to abide in times of threat and fear, of thirst for solitude such as Jesus himself knew in times of need to pray. I cannot help but think also of Thomas the disciple, when he finally saw the Lord after his resurrection – and Jesus invited him, saying 'put your hand into my side'. Here, finally, is the place to hide us in. Within the wounded body of Christ.

And so we are back where we began, beside that wounded, broken body in the silent dark. It is the place where our Christian journey started, as we came to know other Christians. Now, though, we see with new eyes that our place within the body was a refuge, yes; a hiding place, certainly; but above all a base or starting point from which to make known to others the good news. How strange it is to return to where we began and find it so different, so charged with meaning!

A prayer for the resurrection

Lord Jesus,
you rose in triumph from the darkness of death;
help me to live my life in the light of your resurrection,
so that in all I do, and say, and am,
the beauty of your truth may shine:
in your name I make this prayer. Amen.

Questions

1 Why are people afraid of the dark?
2 What do you think happened inside the tomb?
3 Do you ever find it difficult to affirm the resurrection?
4 Is it helpful, and is it right, to commemorate loved ones who have died? And if so, how?
5 Have you ever found insights into the meaning of the resurrection in unexpected ways or places?

2

Ascension

---◆━◆◆━---

Luke 24.36–51, RSV

As they were saying this, Jesus himself stood among them. But they were startled and frightened, and supposed that they saw a spirit. And he said to them, 'Why are you troubled, and why do questionings rise in your hearts? See my hands and my feet, that it is I myself; handle me, and see; for a spirit has not flesh and bones as you see that I have.' And while they still disbelieved for joy, and wondered, he said to them, 'Have you anything here to eat?' They gave him a piece of broiled fish, and he took it and ate before them. Then he said to them, 'These are my words which I spoke to you, while I was still with you, that everything written about me in the law of Moses and the prophets and the psalms must be fulfilled.' Then he opened their minds to understand the scriptures, and said to them, 'Thus it is written, that the Christ should suffer and on the third day rise from the dead, and that repentance and forgiveness of sins should be preached in his name to all nations, beginning from Jerusalem. You are witnesses of these things. And behold, I send the promise of my Father upon you; but stay in the city, until you are clothed with power from on high.' Then he led them out as far as Bethany, and lifting up his hands he blessed them. While he blessed them, he parted from them, and was carried up into heaven.

Romans 10.5–9, RSV

Moses writes that the man who practises the righteousness which is based on the law shall live by it. But the righteousness based on faith says, Do not say in your heart, 'Who will ascend into heaven?' (that is, to bring Christ down) or 'Who will descend into the abyss?' (that is, to bring Christ up from the dead). But what does it say? The word is near you, on your lips and in your heart (that is, the word

of faith which we preach); because, if you confess with your lips
that Jesus is Lord and believe in your heart that God raised him
from the dead, you will be saved.

The Ascension is unique among the glorious mysteries in being
described twice by the same writer, Luke. He tells of Jesus' departure
into heaven at the end of his Gospel; and then again at the beginning
of the Acts of the Apostles. The slightly less familiar version is given
here. The other is to be found at Acts 1.1–11. In the last chapter,
praying the resurrection turned out to involve an unexpected mixture
of light and joy, darkness and fear together. This is partly because, at
this stage of the glorious mysteries, the resurrection is still something
which happened miraculously, once, to someone else. In this next
stage of the prayer, we are still dealing with something we think we
know very well, but – just as before – a little probing will be enough
to show us that we are still only skimming the surface of the truth.
We have looked at some of the rituals associated with ongoing reverence for the mortal remains of loved ones. We have now to consider
how it feels and what it means for us to experience bereavement, and
sometimes the additional impact of having no mortal remains of our
loved ones left to honour.

In the previous chapter, I mentioned the parish churches of this
country, which are among our most familiar, and often most neglected,
landmarks. Much more recent, almost as familiar and equally dis-
regarded, are our war memorials. In every population centre, and
in many schools, colleges and work places, the names of those who
died in the World Wars of the twentieth century are recorded
individually on tablets or walls, or other forms of inscription. Most
of the time those names go unnoticed; but it is a common practice
to read out the names on Remembrance Day. We do this each year
at the college in Cambridge where I am Dean. One of the students
of the college took his interest in the names a great deal further than
that, and researched the college's war dead as individuals, visiting
their graves overseas, discovering Victoria Crosses and other awards
for conspicuous courage, bringing many of those names to life and
reminding us that they were real people once, just like us. It was one
of the cruellest side effects of the two World Wars that the bodies
of those war dead were not brought home. Many families had no
funeral, no grave, nowhere to weep, no place to beautify with gifts

of flowers each Flower Sunday. This was the situation in which the friends and family of Jesus found themselves after he departed from their sight. As the reading states, 'he parted from them, and was carried up into heaven'.

It is impossible for us to see the picture as they must have seen it. We know what lies around the corner, the miracle of Pentecost, when God poured out the Holy Spirit on the apostles. We know that they were inspired by that miraculous gift to do deeds of extraordinary courage, faith and love. But back then that was a lot further than they themselves could see. Their friend, brother, teacher had died, and had appeared to them after death, restored to a new but mysterious and 'other' form of life. But they were not yet ready, any more than we are ready now, for the fullness of divine love to lighten upon them.

Their Lord had left them first through his dying, and now he did so again by his ascending into heaven. That ascending must, at the time, have seemed another, perhaps equally painful, bereavement. True, he had blessed them, and promised them his gift. But then he had spoken during his years of ministry about the resurrection, and that had been no comfort, no bulwark against the terror and grief of loss at his death on the cross. They had heard his words, but the right time was not yet, and they had not understood those words. And as a consequence they could take no comfort from them. Ironically, Jesus had anticipated that this moment of his Ascension was the sign which his followers were hoping for to prove that they were on the right track, following the real Lord (John 6.62). But like so much of what we wish for, when it came the moment was not entirely what they had anticipated it to be.

How often in our lives the key to understanding is to wait for the *right time* (the Bible uses the special term *kairos* for such a time). Only through long experience do we learn not to rush, not to hurry, not to snatch at understanding, but to wait until the moment comes when it is right to speak or act. Jesus was gone, and it must have seemed that now, finally, he was lost to them for ever. It is helpful to pause here, to think briefly about what they would have expected for Jesus after he was taken from their sight. For there was controversy then, just as nowadays, about whether such a thing as life after death could exist. Jesus himself in the Gospels confronted the Sadducees, who did not believe in a resurrection; and his teachings, scattered through the Gospel records, are very clear in telling of life after this life in which we are still who we always were, yet no longer according to the norms of earthly life. He also taught clearly that there is reward in the next life for those who have lived righteously in this one, and punishment for those who have not.

The Old Testament is scattered with references to a shadowy insubstantial place called 'Sheol', where the shades of the dead continue in an insubstantial existence. This is very similar to the world of the dead imagined in Homer's *Odyssey* and visited by the Greek hero Odysseus; a different land, with a different culture, but written around the same time as much of the Old Testament, and holding to a similar conception of life after death. What Odysseus discovered in his encounter with the shades of the dead in the Underworld was a wretched state of semi-existence. The bitterness of it drew from the great hero Achilles, after all his marvellous feats of valour, a cry of hopeless misery:

> Do not speak lightly to me of death, glorious Odysseus!
> I wish I might work as a serf labouring for another man,
> as one with no land of his own and a pittance to live on;
> better that than lording it here over the perished dead.

So says the shade of Achilles to Odysseus (Homer, *Odyssey*, 11.488–491, my translation). And his bitter cry expresses exactly the same view as that of the writer of the Bible book Ecclesiastes: 'A living dog is better than a dead lion' (9.4, RSV).

In this view, whether of ancient Greece or Old Testament Judaism, there is no joy after death, and no hope that one can remain in any worthwhile sense 'oneself'. There are fragmentary allusions in the Psalms to an abode of the dead which is blessed and beautiful, but they are difficult to understand. There is a single unambiguous description of resurrection and judgement at the end of Daniel (12.2). That is all. This is not the place to look for a clear and certain message of hope. For that we must turn to the New Testament. We have to ask ourselves: what exactly *is* the message of the sayings of Jesus? And the interpretation of that message by Paul? Remember that Paul isn't really interested in Jesus' teachings and sayings and healing miracles. He is completely focused on the meaning which is bound up in the resurrection, and its implications for us. The Ascension is, therefore, the pivotal moment when the resurrection appearances of Jesus must come to an end: when the presence of God's Son is taken away and we have to wait for what is to come, to wait 'in sure and certain hope' that the resurrection of Christ means something for us too.

If only that were true. If only our hope were so 'sure and certain'. The truth is that most of us do not rest our Christian faith on the resurrection; and so we struggle to find meaning in the Ascension which follows it. We have become too preoccupied with Jesus as the example of true godliness, the teacher, the healer, the man of prayer and sign. Important though it is to take Jesus as our model for how to live a good life, and for the standard of our behaviour, we should never lose sight of the fact that he is infinitely more than this. Unless we keep both elements together (Jesus the sacrifice for sin and Jesus the example of godly life) there will be little possibility of thinking in a fully complete way about the underlying meaning of Jesus' Ascension – the belief, all woven into one crystalline light of glory, that death is but the threshold into a new way of being. Whenever Jesus pictured life after this life in his preaching and teaching, it was not a shadowy or insubstantial existence but a thing of riches, light and glory. And above all, a place of truth. In that next life, our way of being in this life will be subject to divine scrutiny. We shall have to give an account of what we have done with the talents entrusted to us.

At this point, after some consideration of how to proceed, I have to pause and change direction a little. For it was at this point in the writing of this little book that my words and thoughts and arguments turned into a pressing and painful reality. My mother died. It happened suddenly and unexpectedly. She fell ill on Christmas Day, 2010, and after being given every kind of care and treatment for several weeks in hospital to no avail, it was finally agreed between us that her life support should be switched off. The morning after the decision had been made, all the close family gathered, some after driving hundreds of miles through the night. We stood around her bedside – my father, my brother and sister, my mother's sister, brother and sister-in-law. The nursing staff did what they had to do as gently and self-effacingly as possible, shutting off the machines which were doing the work her own body no longer could; and then they left us alone together in her room. For nearly an hour we watched her final, reflexive, purely physical continuation of breathing, each intake of air seeming that it would, it *must*, be her last. The minutes ticked by. Her breathing became shallower and more intermittent; yet still a pulse beat on in her neck, moment after moment, signalling the surprising tenacity of a body whose soul was letting go. And we waited for the cessation of those movements of breath and pulse which would give us permission to say the unthinkable, the unimaginable – that this woman who had meant so much, to so many, for so long, had let go of life at last.

It was an experience of collective grief and agony – no other word will do – such as I have never experienced before; and it is still too raw, much too raw, for me to add much detail yet to what I can express of that terrible pain. But one thing I can say with a power of conviction which is nothing to do with wishful thinking; which came to me in my desperate suffering with a power destructive of all doubt and fear: 'I *know* that my Redeemer liveth' (Job 19.25, AV). And another verse of Scripture had sunk even more firmly into the depths of my being in those anxious weeks beforehand, and stayed with me even there in that pivotal moment of pain. Indeed it is with me still, echoing in my thoughts and winning for me a peace and courage entirely from without, for my own reserves have been drained utterly dry. Paul wrote to those oh-so-clever Corinthians of the wonders of the life to come, the life which had been promised them. He spread before them his vision of that world to come – 'O death, where is thy sting? O grave, where is thy victory?' (1 Corinthians 15.55, AV). At the end he summed up the encouragement *and* the vision in this single, simple phrase: 'in the Lord your labour is not in vain' (1 Corinthians 15.58, RSV). Over and over again those words went through my mind, night after night as I sat by my mother's bedside and watched and waited, in a silence and isolation like the women at the foot of the cross – waiting for a death they wanted to come quickly, and also not to come at all. 'In the Lord your labour is not in vain,' said the Scripture, and I believed and therefore I hoped. A little later, it is possible for me to begin reflecting on that time of letting go, as I have done here, but only with a mental flinching at the mere thought of having to revisit it, and with a huge effort at self-control to hold back the grief just enough to enable me to write about it.

In the course of my Christian life, I have fallen into a habit of using Scripture in two ways. There is my academic habit of questioning

2 mass of
reads ... of bible

and analysing Scripture, asking questions about why the text was written, to whom, about its theological aims. This feeds my mind in its inquiries, giving me the understanding I need to do the job I do, to support others in their journeys in faith, to underpin and feed my own.

Then there is my other way of using Scripture, the way which is not about the mind and its inquiring, but about the quest for another kind of truth, a truth which, in a different way, is equally fruitful and rewarding – that is, through prayer. In the latter case, I prefer to settle on a few words and let them sink into me to do their work, like a health-giving medicine. As I write, the Lenten prayer 'make me a clean heart' (Psalm 51.12; also 73.13; and Proverbs 20.9; my translation) is at the centre of my daily prayers. I did not choose the words, they chose me as I sat at evening prayer in the college chapel. This is often how the prayers we really need are gifted to us by God. We can have confidence that this is reasonable because we know from centuries of testing that it works. The words, being Scripture, are more than just a record of the past – they are both message and witness to the present. Through the Holy Spirit they spoke to me in my bereavement, so that I could, I can, find the strength to endure – 'in the Lord your labour is not in vain'. In the same way they have spoken to countless others. It is no coincidence that God's Son was revealed to us as 'the Word'. We needed to *hear* him. We still do.

So I am now, as I write, in that same state of separation as the disciples faced after the Ascension – a state of part-knowledge and part-hope, mixed with grief and confusion, but somehow within that a sublime, exalted state of hope. This is not a book, though, about coping with bereavement. I have only mentioned my experience to show how suddenly and unexpectedly the beliefs which simmer away in the back of our faithful minds can come to the forefront of our thinking, and begin to predominate in our thoughts and actions. We can read and reflect on these meanings, perhaps on our own, perhaps as part of a group. We can reflect slowly during and after Easter, or at other times of the year. Most of us have at some time faced this intersection of belief with personal experience, and found that belief cannot still or silence the questioning. In the shocks of letting go of loved ones, there are always regrets and might-have-beens, there is always a wondering about whether it could all have turned out differently, had we only done *X* or said *Y*. The key thing, in all this, is to reassure ourselves not with foolish delusions but with a 'reasonable, religious, and holy hope', as the writer Jeremy Taylor puts it in a remarkable seventeenth-century prayer. The pain we feel in letting go of loved ones (whether we believe it is only for a little while [John 14.19] or for eternity) is indivisible from the inexpressible joy of having loved them, and of loving them still. Who could wish to lessen the pain of letting go by instead embracing the only realistic alternative (given that death is something all of us must face), namely, never to have experienced the love with which that pain and grief are inextricably bound up? A life without such pain could only be possible if that life were also empty of love. The price of painless peace of mind, it seems to me, is far too high.

Whatever Jesus had taught or said or done, and whatever hope he had given to his disciples during his lifetime, that moment of departure was a final fracture: an end to the familiarity and custom of their daily relationship. No more turning to him to answer their questions or resolve their doubts. No more luxuriating in the simple closeness of someone who mattered to them, and they to him. In his physical presence he was gone from them, and they were left waiting: waiting for . . . they did not know what. So now, if we meditate on the Ascension, if we read and absorb the story, and picture ourselves as part of the scene, how do we imagine it? When I imagine how it must have been, I usually discover myself as one of those staring at the place from which Jesus has just departed: rather like when you wave goodbye to someone who is leaving on a train or by car – you wave until that moment comes with a *snap!* when they vanish from view, and are gone. And there is a moment, perhaps several moments, when you stare at the place where you glimpsed them for the last time. Then comes the turning point when you make the move, uncomfortable with the finality of the gesture, and walk away, back to the business of life. In the case of a bereavement, the person is constantly in your thoughts; your loved one's image shimmers before you at unexpected moments. Your sense of loss is bubbling away under the surface, sometimes exploding out (usually at inconvenient and embarrassing times) like a volcano which looks dormant but then turns out to be very much active. It is an experience which brings us to the threshold between life and death through its very intensity and power. And from this liminal position we can look both ways, back into our past and forward into a promised future.

When we start contemplating our most painful experiences of separation and loss in personal relationships, we find that they are usually a most extreme form of our perpetual human experience of *change* and *letting go* of the past. We can begin with two undeniable historical facts. First, we know for sure that the human person Jesus once lived and walked the earth, complete with a real, mortal, human body. What happened to that human body when he died? Scripture traces two stages. After the tomb was empty, Jesus appeared in a body which was recognizably his *as it had once been*; and he spoke (to Mary; to Thomas; to others) and behaved (he ate with his disciples; he provided food for them; he taught them) like the man they had known before.

There is no reason to suppose that back then they were any more *predisposed* to believe in the resurrection of a human being from death than we are today. Sceptical disbelief was their default setting, as it is also ours. The equally plain second historical fact is that there are no material relics of Jesus, and no credible records of his body remaining upon earth. From the beginning, Christians were distinctive for caring with special scrupulosity for the bodies of their dead. They gave particularly diligent care to the bodies of martyrs, i.e. those who died witnessing to their faith under threat of pain or death. The remains of martyrs became, for those first Christians, a guarantee of the holiness of places of worship, a means of binding all the faithful under the powerful protection of the martyrs' prayers. Martyrs' relics were traded between bishops who wanted to found churches. They were fought over because of the trade and prosperity and honour which they could attract to one place or another. Bones, hair, clothing, possessions – all might be treasured up and handed on. Many would be faked. The followers of St Francis kept as a precious relic of that holy man a fragment of parchment on which the saint himself had written. There is no reason to doubt the genuineness of that written fragment. The Turin Shroud, on the other hand, is a notorious example of a relic which has attracted both reverence and scepticism. A few years ago I visited the city of Lucca in Italy, where there is another famous relic called the *Volto Santo* or 'Holy Face' – a wooden carving of the face of the crucified Christ which goes back to the eighth century at least, and which has been venerated for over

29

The disciples didn't believe no tomb for Jesus – no record Later all kinds a thousand years as the work of Nicodemus, an image made from the actual face of Jesus.

Only a few relics are associated with Jesus, and none claimed to be remains of his adult body. Norwich Cathedral attracted pilgrims when it managed to acquire a relic of the precious blood of Jesus in 1171.[1] Several churches claimed to possess the foreskin removed at his circumcision. There are also cloths, not just the shroud of Turin, but also the cloth used to wipe his face on the way to Calvary. There are relics which were said to be from the Passion – the crown of thorns, the wood and nails used in the crucifixion – all of which claim the honour of contact with his body. But nothing is left of the actual body which was taken down from the cross.

The truth is, there was no demand for earthly remains of Jesus, because there was no supply. The witness of Scripture is completely clear and straightforward on this point. As Acts puts it, extremely succinctly, 'he was lifted up, and a cloud took him out of their sight' (Acts 1.9, RSV). There was nothing left to provide a focal point for their sense of loss. And in that situation, they had nothing to do but wait and hope. If they believed in the resurrection as Jesus taught it, they still had no fixed ideas about the timing; and the first thing anyone wants to know when they are promised a blessing, or any kind of good, is, '*When* will I receive it?' Believing that our separation from those we love will not be eternal does not in any way insulate us from suffering when we are forced apart for a period of time the duration of which we have no means of telling. 'Jam tomorrow' is no substitute for 'jam today'.

The resurrection mystery began by showing how death changes our world and tears holes in it. The Ascension stands for that painful experience of apparently final separation – when the body of the one who has died, and the persons of those who live on, are consigned to separate realms for an unspecified period. The ability to touch, see, hear, smell the other person is taken away. And old habits of touch, sight, hearing, and even smell, die hard. Even clearing out a loved one's clothes can bring them vividly to our mind's eye as the scent of them makes its abrupt and painful impact on us.

---

[1] Nicholas Vincent, *The Holy Blood: King Henry III and the Westminster blood relic* (Cambridge: Cambridge University Press, 2001), p. 70.

The Gospel story of Jesus, we have to remind ourselves here, is not an identikit model for our own pattern of life. There is no suggestion that after we are buried we shall immediately be resurrected and appear to those who love us. The meaning of Jesus' resurrection and Ascension, then, is much more than a simple indicator of what will happen to us after death. In ordinary life, as opposed to the extraordinary story of Jesus, the moment of final separation between the living and the dead normally happens at the end of the funeral service, when the body is *committed*, either to the ground – 'earth to earth' – or to be cremated – 'ashes to ashes, dust to dust'. Then those who grieve must turn their backs and walk away for the last time, leaving those mortal remains to their resting place, making that final break with the past. It is an extraordinarily brave and painful thing to do, that act of turning and walking away. For Christians and for non-believers alike, it is a giant leap of faith that life must and will go on, and that we must begin to encounter the world again and make sense of it afresh without the presence of the person now departed this life.

Within this fragment of the story of Jesus, there is hidden a truth so huge that we almost do not dare to look at it. It is rarely acknowledged or spoken about in the faith today. When we hear the last words of Jesus to his disciples (Luke 24.46–47), and then Luke tells us of the moment of his Ascension (Acts 1.9), what we are receiving is a prophecy and its fulfilment together. What this fact reveals is the reality of divine providence – we might call it 'God's fore-thought' for the world. What this means is that Christian faith has a *purpose*, not just on the level of our individual lives, but on a global scale: 'God our Saviour . . . desires everyone to be saved and to come to the knowledge of the truth' (1 Timothy 2.3–4, NRSV). Thus it becomes clear that Christian history also has a *meaning*, and that we can come to understand that meaning. The Gospels are full of foretellings and fulfilments, which witness to a sense of divine providence at work in apparently meaningless events. I have just mentioned one – the prophecy by Jesus of his own resurrection 'after three days'. This is referred to several times in the Gospel records. It is also specified in this speech as something foretold both by the Old Testament prophets ('thus it is written') and by Jesus himself. But there are several other prophecies made here (not to mention countless others in Scripture), all of which, as we read them, we know to have been fulfilled:

Repentance and forgiveness of sins should be preached in his name to all nations, beginning from Jerusalem. You are witnesses of these things . . . I send the promise of my Father upon you; but stay in the city, until you are clothed with power from on high.

(Luke 24.47–49, RSV)

The preaching of repentance and forgiveness is referred to as something foretold in Scripture; but their being witnesses, receiving the Father's promise and being clothed with power, are all prophecies declared by the Lord himself.

The fulfilment of prophecy is at the very heart of Christian belief. It enabled the first disciples to make sense of the death, resurrection and Ascension of their friend Jesus. Their sense that God was at work in these events was so strong that they were certain God would have left guidance as to their meaning in the sacred writings of the Jewish people. In believing this, they were not doing anything very extraordinary. In every generation but our own, people have been sure that God has written his nature and essence into the fabric of the world, and made his intentions for his Creation and his chosen people plain in certain sacred writings. The words of these texts, absorbed through worship, study and prayer, come to life in us and speak to us, so that we can make the Ascension our own, just as we did the resurrection. There is nothing to fear; and even when we are afraid, in the Scriptures there is that 'sure and certain hope'[2] to be received by all who are willing.

This is not difficult for us to accept in theory, at least not for ourselves as people who are already within the Church, already members of the body of Christ. But we also have to remember that our most precious, holy book, the Bible, is not a book which everyone accepts as sacred or understands as containing the keys to 'salvation' (in the proper sense of the word, namely to reach, or be given, safety and refuge and healing). The certainty of former centuries, the conviction of Christian truth, the knowledge of the power of Christian faith, all these things have been thrown into doubt in our own time. No longer can we rely on an assumption of moral or spiritual superiority. No longer can we dismiss those outside the faith as 'heathen' or 'unbelievers', 'unchristian' or 'unchurched'. We have come, gradually,

---

[2] From the Burial of the Dead, BCP 1662.

reluctantly, awkwardly, to see that our faith is not shared by many, and to accept that what is right for us may not be right for them.

Here is a great difficulty for all Christians. For we are a missionary people. It is long overdue that we should set aside outdated images of missionaries as 'do-gooders' going to faraway lands to patronize native peoples and obliterate their culture. That kind of mission has come to seem improper and oppressive. Still the fact remains that our faith is one which we are called to *share*, and which we ought to be *eager* to share. The moment of the Ascension is certainly a moment of separation and loss; but it is also a new beginning – the moment when the disciples become the body of Christ on earth. Now that his physical body has been lifted up, those disciples and witnesses of the Ascension must become his feet travelling to spread the gospel: 'How beautiful upon the mountains are the feet of him who brings good tidings, who publishes peace' (Isaiah 52.7, RSV).

They must become his hands reaching out to heal, as the apostle urges: 'Rekindle the gift of God that is within you through the laying on of my hands' (2 Timothy 1.6, RSV).

They must become his heart bearing and showing the love of God for all his children, as Paul again tells them:

> My conscience bears me witness in the Holy Spirit, that I have great sorrow and unceasing anguish in my heart. For I could wish that I myself were accursed and cut off from Christ for the sake of my brethren, my kinsmen by race.   (Romans 9.1–3, RSV)

What does it mean for us Christians today to be the feet, the hands, the heart of Christ in the world? Surely it cannot be anything to do with bullying or patronizing others into believing! The Ascension is a challenge to us, to rediscover what it means for all human beings to be made in the image and likeness of God (Genesis 1.26) by starting with the basics. With ourselves, in other words. By modelling our lives and actions, words and thoughts, after the image and likeness of Christ. His physical presence is no longer with us to proclaim the good news, to bring healing and divine compassion. But we are ready to do his will, to make real his ongoing presence. Our feet can be swift to bring the gospel. Our hands prepared to reach out to those in need, with practical help and unselfconscious kindness. Our hearts filled with divine compassion, and so being delighted, honoured, to serve Christ by serving others, and learning to love as he loves us. For Christians, thank God, *motivation* is everything. It isn't enough to do the right thing for the wrong reason – we have to want to do the right thing for the right reason. We have to do good to others because we are sure that God loves them as much as he does us; and because we have recognized the divine image and likeness in them. Putting the needs of others first, whether feeding the hungry, tending the sick or sharing the good news with the lost and vulnerable, is a way of being Christlike.

This way of thinking represents real (which is to say 'Christlike') Christianity. It is intensely practical, free of dogma, doctrine, legalism, perfectionism. Most of all it is centred not on self-fulfilment or self-aggrandizement, neither on judgement or judgementalism, but on identifying, and tending to, the needs of others.

This understanding of what it means to be a Christian, a part of the body of Christ, is very different from how some Christian communities understand themselves. Their lives may be centred on getting their beliefs into the correct style and formulation; on being clear about who's saved and who isn't by drawing up Terms and Conditions; and on making converts to the faith because in the end those who do not believe are damned to hell and to eternal punishment.

In essence, this point about right motivation being the thing that really matters is shared by good people within and outside the Christian faith. Rabbi Lionel Blue has expressed the same idea in a slightly different way, by saying that righteous people are those who look after their own souls and other people's bodies, while hypocrites are those who look after their own body and other people's souls. Yes indeed!

So the Ascension challenges us to rethink our assumptions about what it is that God wants of us. We are no longer able to hide behind excuses that we cannot be sure how we ought to live, or what it is that the life of faith requires. Jesus has told us clearly that we are to witness to him, and that we shall receive power to carry out whatever he requires of us. Thus his Ascension marks the point when the disciples become *doers* of the word, and not *hearers* only (James 1.22). We shall have to probe further into divine providence and the meaning of salvation before this journey is over.

A prayer for the Ascension

Lord Jesus, by your ascension,
you drew my mind up into heavenly places,
inspiring me to dedicate my life
to serving you wherever I find you in others:
strengthen my resolve to seek and serve you,
and my trust in your loving purposes.
In your name I make this prayer. Amen.

Questions

1 Why did Jesus have to leave us?
2 What does his Ascension mean for you?
3 Should bereavement be painful for a Christian who believes in life after this life?
4 What is the point of funerals?
5 If life in this world has a special meaning and purpose for Christians, how should we share that belief?

3

Pentecost

———◆•◆•◆———

Acts 2.1–4, RSV

When the day of Pentecost had come, they were all together in one place. And suddenly a sound came from heaven like the rush of a mighty wind, and it filled all the house where they were sitting. And there appeared to them tongues as of fire, distributed and resting on each one of them. And they were all filled with the Holy Spirit and began to speak in other tongues, as the Spirit gave them utterance.

1 Corinthians 12.4–11, RSV

Now there are varieties of gifts, but the same Spirit; and there are varieties of service, but the same Lord; and there are varieties of working, but it is the same God who inspires them all in every one. To each is given the manifestation of the Spirit for the common good. To one is given through the Spirit the utterance of wisdom, and to another the utterance of knowledge according to the same Spirit, to another faith by the same Spirit, to another gifts of healing by the one Spirit, to another the working of miracles, to another prophecy, to another the ability to distinguish between spirits, to another various kinds of tongues, to another the interpretation of tongues. All these are inspired by one and the same Spirit, who apportions to each one individually as he wills.

The glorious mysteries are a prayer centred on Christ. Everything and everyone else who appears in the five sections of the prayer is included because of what they reveal to us about the truth of God through the person of Jesus, his Son, the Messiah. This stage of the prayer is the moment when our thoughts turn to pondering the question of *how* God makes himself known to us. It is often said that Christianity is a historical faith. I have said as much myself, in this book. By this we mean that it is founded upon real things which really happened to real people in real time. And that is indeed the case. This sounds like a positive, and in fact it is, at least for the most part. The power of the Christian story has endured over centuries, as the power of the Jewish story did before it. We know who we are because our story tells us so. The danger is that we become so used to thinking of our faith as historical (in other words, rooted in what has happened in the past) that we forget that Christianity is also a very future-oriented, innovative faith. The early Christians were very sensitive to the contrast between what is seen, as *perishable*, and what is not seen, as *eternal*. They knew that they must put their energy into things which would draw them closer in love to God, whether by prayer, worship, teaching or service. Perhaps our hearts have become a little too focused on things which will not last, so that we risk forgetting there is an eternal perspective too. Sometimes it is good for us to attempt what we know is really impossible, by trying, through prayer, to see ourselves in the perspective of eternity. We shall not succeed, but we shall gain a sense of the wonderful love of God, and the miracle of his reaching out to restore us to divine life, which was his original plan for us.

In turning to the giving of the Holy Spirit at Pentecost, we encounter something, or some*one*, who is both new and utterly familiar, ancient and yet fresh, different. That paradox is typical of how we meet with the Holy Spirit. Thus far, I have been offering encouragement to meditate on each mystery; but the descent of the Holy Spirit upon the disciples at Pentecost, which turned them into apostles, men 'sent out' to spread the gospel, makes meditation (picturing the subject matter of the prayer, imagining the scene) more of a challenge:

> The wind blows where it chooses, and you hear the sound of it, but you do not know where it comes from or where it goes. So it is with everyone who is born of the Spirit. (John 3.8, NRSV)

> As yet there was no Spirit, because Jesus was not yet glorified. (John 7.39, NRSV)

The Holy Spirit is the third 'person' of the Trinity. 'Trinity' is the word we Christians use to define God as we understand him, and as we have learned to know him. It is not a word in ordinary use (and this is true for the original Latin and the Greek as well as the English form of the word 'Trinity') – it has only ever meant 'God as three persons but one being'. It was a word invented by Christians, because they could not find anything in the ordinary languages of their day which did justice to the reality of God as they experienced him in Christ. Language could not keep pace with the impetus of their discoveries about God's real essence; so language had to be *made up* to catch up.

Because 'Trinity' is a technical term, we have to learn what it means through listening, absorbing and accepting it as part of Christian history – in much the same way as our identity as part of a blood family comes to us through learning, and re-enacting, its customs. We find our place within the common life of our blood family, and our church family, through a process of time passing and experience shared. The label we use for the third person of the Trinity, that familiar title 'Holy Spirit', is rather like the term 'Trinity' itself – it is a title which does not draw its meaning from other usages – it only means what it means primarily. This is very different from the other two 'persons' of the Trinity, the Father and the Son. It does not matter that 'no one has ever seen God' (1 John 4.12, NRSV) because we all know what a 'father' is; and whether our own experience of 'father' is good or not, we still know what a good father is *supposed* to be. The same is true of 'Son'. We may not all have sons, or be sons, but we know what sons are – we know the primary application of the word, and we have an ideal, general, image of it in our minds.

Not so with 'Holy Spirit' and 'Trinity'. They just mean what they *specifically* mean. So our task as Christians is to encounter the Holy Spirit (which is how we come to realize that God is more than just the Father, and more than the Father and the Son together) and from then to discover the Trinity; and to work out the meaning of the *terms* and *labels* from our experience of the *realities* – just as we once did with 'fathers' and 'God the Father', and with 'sons' and 'God the Son'.

I hope this way of beginning will help us to see that we must learn who the Holy Spirit is from observing how the Holy Spirit works. 'Holy Spirit' has been brilliantly described, in a phrase I have used already, as 'the go-between God'.[1] It took longer for the Church to

---

[1] John V. Taylor, in his book *The Go-Between God* (London: SCM Press, second edition 2004).

nail the identity and essence of the Holy Spirit than of the Father
and Son precisely because the first Christians had the same problem
as we do. We know we experience glimpses of glory and moments
of encounter and presence (what I described, borrowing from a
theologian called Rudolf Otto, in my book *Joyful Christianity* as 'the
numinous'), but those experiences are not reducible to mere words.
So how can we make sense of the go-between God, the Holy Spirit,
who is the agent at work in our encounters with the divine presence
in daily life?

We need not worry that we cannot actually define the Holy Spirit.
Jesus once told his disciples that they would be able to tell what was
from God and what was not by judging according to results: 'you
will know them by their fruits' (Matthew 7.16, 20, NRSV). This will
be our guide. It is not the aim of this book to explain the Holy Spirit
in terms of abstract theology, but to challenge readers to recognize
the Holy Spirit in practical terms, as they encounter him every day.
The point of prayer – any prayer, not just the glorious mysteries – is
to emerge from our time of encounter with God able to see more
clearly what was always before us; to 'know more truly the greatness
of God's love', as the 1928 Prayer Book puts it. The Holy Spirit is the
one who turns our offerings and efforts in prayer into communica-
tions and encounters. The Holy Spirit is the one who makes us aware
that God is calling us, that God wants us, that we are precious to
God.

More than a millennium and a half has gone by since Christians
decided that they were clear who the Holy Spirit is, and so first
gathered up all our perceptions of the truth of God into that one
being, God the Holy Trinity. In the intervening time, we have lost
touch with the sheer mystery and the struggle involved in how that
understanding was reached. As I just said, this is not the place to list
every step of the theological discussions and the devotional searchings
which led to that eventual truth. One revelation alone will be enough
for now. It came to a Greek bishop called Gregory, towards the end
of the fourth century AD, and it enabled him, and the Church, to
formulate the final version of the Nicene Creed which so many
Christians pray each Sunday in their worship. Gregory realized that
God did not just plonk the whole content of holy truth in front of
us and expect us to accept it, and to make sense of it. If we get too
much material to cope with in one go, we are all too prone to reject

it just to simplify matters! Instead, God, being a God of history, let time do the job. So, Gregory argued, God revealed himself to his people as Father in the Old Testament, as Son in the New Testament and as Holy Spirit *in the Church*. Church, therefore, is what God has given us to stop us making the Bible into our golden calf (Exodus 32) – he is the God of the living, not of the dead (Mark 12.27); of the Spirit, not the letter (2 Corinthians 3.6). It is the specific function of the Holy Spirit to lead us into all that truth which we were not yet ready to bear when Jesus the Son finally ascended to his Father; at the time when it is right for each portion of the truth to be revealed (Romans 5.6). So Christianity is not a static or timeless faith; quite the reverse. It depends completely upon an understanding of God revealing himself in human time to human beings, progressively.

As a parish priest, I firmly believed in keeping church buildings open, so that they could be used for peace and prayer by anyone who needed them. This entailed a certain amount of risk – it made us more vulnerable to vandalism and to theft. What was the alternative? A church that is locked all day is no more than a museum! It is dedicated only to preserving the past, not to shaping the living for the needs of the future. The same is true of our faith. All Christian people recognize the precious treasure which has been entrusted to us down the centuries. But we are specifically forbidden to bury that treasure in the ground where it can stay safe but *do* nothing (Matthew 25.27). We are not supposed to make church buildings into places protected *from* people. Neither should we make our church customs into a barrier wall which people who come seeking God are unable to climb. The treasures of the gospel are for everyone.

This simple gospel truth that what is old is always being discovered anew, and made new, turns out to help us understand the very heart of God. It is a source of perpetual human frustration that for each generation, having discovered the hard way (through personal experience) what the truths are that matter in life (about how to behave and what to set your heart on), it turns out to be impossible to persuade those who follow in the next generation to accept these hard-won truths. Each generation has to learn for itself, by experience and not just through being told, what are the things which matter. So each generation must rediscover God afresh in ways which are both old and new. God is the 'ancient of days', but he is also the one who says 'I make all things new' (Daniel 7.9, RSV; Revelation

21.5, AV and RSV). God revealed himself as a Father in the Old Testament, and as a Son in the New; but before our eyes and in our own time he is here as the Holy Spirit in our world today, building things up, inspiring, giving courage, affirming, guiding and comforting us. He is that person of the Trinity who brings our faith to life and keeps it lively. He leads us into all the truth (John 16.13).

All this makes it sound so easy, the ideas so clear, the way so obvious. I know that the reality can be very different. Our faith is not as strong and confident as it ought to be. We may believe that we received the Holy Spirit at our baptism and yet feel unconnected to it, unable to listen to the Holy Spirit's voice. All too often there is a deep rift between what we think should be the case about ourselves, and how we inwardly *feel* about ourselves. We can speak the language of human beings as made in the image of God, as being loved and valued by God. But we can still feel, within ourselves, unworthy, distant from God, broken and banished from the divine circle of love. This is shockingly common. Too many people endure, in the everyday business of living, a profound sense of unworthiness. They do not feel that they are made in the divine image. They do not believe in their hearts that God's Holy Spirit is within them as a burning flame. They are convinced that they do not deserve divine love, that by the actions and choices of their life past they have forfeited divine forgiveness. They feel that whenever good things come to them, those blessings are undeserved; whereas whenever they endure suffering, it is no more than a fair return for wrongdoing in the past.

You might think that as a Fellow of a Cambridge college I would be surrounded by capable, brilliant, acute-thinking people who are intelligent enough to recognize their own worth (which, after all, has been affirmed by those who ought to know on multiple occasions – they have sat exam after exam, written theses, defended their views at interview, acquired distinctions and affirmations). Yet despite these repeated confirmations of ability and unbiased evaluations of intelligence, there are still a good number who are firmly convinced that this has happened to them by accident or mistake. The examiners must have muddled their papers up with someone else's. The interviewers probably sent the offer of a Cambridge place to the wrong school. The professors who examined the doctorate doubtless awarded it out of pity rather than esteem. Beliefs of this kind, which continue to be deeply held despite every piece of external evidence to the contrary, constitute one version of a pervasive form of low self-esteem. It is so common in society that psychologists have given it a label. They refer to it as 'impostor syndrome' or 'the impostor phenomenon'.

Bound up in this phenomenon is a bundle of fears – that other people have too high an opinion of your abilities ('They think I can do it, but I can't!'), that the misconception will be discovered ('They will see through me!') and that whatever successes you have achieved ought to be attributed to factors beyond your control, such as luck, rather than to ability or effort ('I'm not really any good at all, I was lucky with the questions; I had to work much harder than I would if I was really talented'). This is the underlying anxiety which drives so much high achievement in our culture. It may also help to explain why those who are the most brilliant, most creative and most high-achieving in our society can also be those who are least satisfied, and most discontented, with the fruits of their labours – perpetually guilty that they have not done enough, that one day people will see their supposed achievements as the card-castles which they really are. Such people pay a high price for their top qualifications and impressive deeds. So, sometimes, do their families, who act as the shock absorbers between them and the world they have to face while secretly, guiltily, feeling that they are frauds.

I have described the face of 'impostor syndrome' I know best: that in the academic world. But it is not by any means to be confined only to university life. Low self-esteem can fuel the same type of distortion in all kinds of personal relationships – with the result that no demonstration of affection from a spouse, or child, or friend, is ever sufficient to comfort our need to fill up the self-esteem deficit with affirmation from outside. Because we are convinced that we are worthless, incapable of real affection or true self-sacrifice, we can even come to reject our own best instincts as misguided or pointless. This emotional version of the impostor phenomenon makes people feel guilty, and then angry, and often then they may become abusive; haunted by feelings of unworthiness, they try to shift the blame for that sense of worthlessness away from themselves, and outwards onto others. In this way, the impostor phenomenon causes untold damage, often passing down the vicious spiral of demand and dissatisfaction from one generation to the next.

What has the Holy Spirit to do with all this? The answer is simple. The impostor phenomenon is a distortion of reality – by twisting our perceptions of ourselves awry it makes it impossible for us to recognize ourselves as we really are. I argued in my earlier books in this series that *recognition* is a key factor in how we come to know the truth of God, and so to see ourselves as we truly are. Recognition is supremely important here, because the Holy Spirit is the go-between God who makes us able to see ourselves, and others, as we truly are – children of God the Father; brothers and sisters of God the Son. The Holy Spirit is so closely bound up with the Truth in John's Gospel that it is sometimes difficult to tell them apart (John 14.17). Jesus tells us that he is the Truth (John 14.6) – and the Holy Spirit leads us straight to him (John 14.26; 16.13). Through this Spirit of truth we can come to see properly at last, and in a clear, undistorted perspective – to see ourselves as God's beloved children; and, as the indivisible concomitant of that realization, to see other people as equally unique, precious and beloved.

Because Christianity is more than just a historical faith (in a backward-looking way), it does not only turn to past wisdom for guidance in making the life choices we face each day. The Holy Spirit is, we have discovered, how God makes himself known to us today. We can expect, and ought to find, that the Holy Spirit opens our eyes to see old things in new ways, and, above all, to discover fresh truth in ancient writings. Within the Christian faith, we rely fundamentally on the Bible for our guide. We believe that Scripture contains everything we need to know in order to be saved. This is a fact those with impostor syndrome need to hear; and that includes anyone who needs convincing that he or she is a worthwhile person, precious to God and truly loved and valued by other people. But believing this does not instantly solve all our problems. We are still faced with decisions about *how* we read the Scriptures as a *guide to truth*. We don't think the Bible's just a history book, never mind just a story book; but on the other hand we can't pretend that every word of it will affirm the accuracy of modern scientific understanding of the world. It is more than a history or story book; but it is not a text-book either. We can't treat it as a set of rules because Jesus our Lord warned us to avoid that over-simplistic approach. We are probably sick and tired of different Christian factions beating each other over the head with proof texts. We need a different plan for reading Scripture, one that enables us to discern the Holy Spirit in the words, and so to trace the pattern of God's activity in the world.

How are we to find confidence in our reading of Scripture? We could hardly make sense of a book as complex and difficult as the Bible without the Holy Spirit to enthuse us with the belief that truth lies within the text, to guide us in our private reading, to encourage us in our corporate encounters with God's word through Christian worship. There is no chance that we could make full sense of it alone. But help is close at hand. There is no need to work it all out from the beginning, because a lot of the groundwork (if not all the detail) was done for us centuries ago. Back in the fifth century AD, not long after Gregory and his brilliant explanation of the Holy Spirit, another bishop, Augustine, wrote a handbook for Christian teachers and preachers. He filled it with good advice about rules and methods for handling the holy books. One simple rule which he set down, and which is still in use today, is that the teacher must use the clear and simple passages to make sense of the arcane and difficult ones. Augustine gave lots of examples as he filled in the details of his teaching plan:

> Scripture asserts nothing that is not the universal faith in matters past, present and future. It tells the story of the past, it foretells the future, it demonstrates the present: but it does all these things to nurture and confirm the same love . . . which is that impulse of the mind to enjoy God for himself, and our neighbour beside God.[2]

Then he boiled it all down to one key tool for judging whether we have understood the text aright: 'Whatever is not consistent with love of God and neighbour cannot be a right interpretation of Scripture.'

Here at last is the key we need to understanding how God makes himself known to us. For this guideline is also still in use today. The only standard we are ultimately allowed, and need, is the standard of love. Love itself is the guide to how the Scriptures speak to us. Love is the tool by which we weed out what is our own emotional and cultural baggage from what really comes from God. Love is the greatest of the three things which last for ever. In the end it has to be our yardstick for judging everything. God is love, so everything communicated by the Holy Spirit must also be love. This holds true for our encounters with Scripture: when we read, and think, and

---

[2] Augustine, *On Christian Teaching*, 3.10.14–16; my translation.

meditate, and finally when we pray. It holds true in our everyday lives, when we see reflections of divine love in the words and actions of others, in the beauty of buildings and landscapes, plants and living things, in the sheer joy of existence. If all this sounds harder work than just being handed a list of rules and told to conform to them, we should not be surprised; it is always easier to conform than to step forward into the unknown with only a 'still, small voice' (1 Kings 19.12, AV) to guide us. Four hundred years ago, Jeremy Taylor remarked that 'Men nowadays love not a Religion that will cost them dear'; much has changed in the world since then, but not that plainly stated truth.

The wind blows where it will, and it has power, but it cannot be seen, except through its effects. The Holy Spirit speaks to us, but rarely in articulate words. Its language is the deepest language: the language which is ours from the first moment of our existence as people in our own right, even from early babyhood. The very word 'infant' means one who does not yet have the power of articulate speech – yet no one could doubt that infants have powerful feelings, or that parents can read those feelings and interpret them. The Spirit's language is the language of inexpressible feeling – of the eyes' attention; of the mouth for tasting and touching and making noise; of the heart and throat for feeling emotion; of the guts (as Hebrew would express it) for fear and awe. We are so word-driven that we have to re-learn the true language of God; like a stroke victim learning to speak again we need to start from scratch, mumbling and mixing up our words, so difficult do we find it to pronounce them correctly. The written word is so privileged in modern society that we have become extremely resistant to recognizing and honouring this spiritual language of divine perception. But without it, we have no means of connecting with God, and no capacity for recognizing God in the world around us.

The root of impostor syndrome is being unable to accept that God dwells in us and abides with us. The sufferer has no confidence, no faith, in the assurance which this glorious mystery insists upon. Christianity is meant to be a faith which sets us free from such anxiety; and yet there are many Christians also who experience an unease about whether they are good enough for God. They may even regard their feelings of unworthiness as an essential part of the expression of their faith (because no human being can ever match up to divine goodness) but are really revealing that faith to be on shaky foundations. Expressing this sense of unworthiness is written into some of our best-known prayers – 'we thine unworthy servants do give thee most humble and hearty thanks...'; 'Lord, I am not worthy to receive you'; 'although we be unworthy, through our manifold sins, to offer unto thee any sacrifice...'[3] Unworthiness has its proper place in the Christian's spiritual vocabulary, but it can become too prominent, and even emerge as a 'catch-all' term encompassing the Christian's feelings of guilt, sin and shame, which set him or her at a distance from divine goodness. In all this, the Holy Spirit acts as the agent of *communication*, helping the individual Christian to see those feelings of worthlessness being transformed into blessed assurance. Then the sense of unworthiness is no longer anything to fear. Instead we learn by gradual experience to accept times when we feel this way as *opportunities* for letting go of the past and of what stands in our way, letting ourselves be re-formed in the divine likeness. Thus those feelings of unworthiness are no longer a sign that we believe we are outsiders who do not truly belong. Rather, they become, through the Holy Spirit, a part of the ongoing process of our growth in Christlikeness.

The message of the first Scripture passage, then, must be that the Holy Spirit is the 'person' of God which (who), above all, *communicates* with humankind. The message of the second is that each of us will both experience and manifest the Holy Spirit in a different way, even though God himself is One. Our talents within, the gifts we receive from without, the actions we take upon ourselves as offerings of love – all these 'are inspired by one and the same Spirit' (1 Corinthians 12.11, RSV). We need not consign 'unworthiness' to a category which belongs in the past, only with our moment or process of conversion. We should not fear the ongoing perceptions we have of the distance between our weak and fallible selves and the infinite goodness of the divine Trinity. Both are a necessary part of an ongoing dialogue with God as, through prayer, we move deeper into the ultimate reality of his being.

---

[3] From the General Thanksgiving, BCP 1662; words at the receiving of Communion, *Common Worship* (London, Church House Publishing, 2000), p. 180; from the prayer after Communion, BCP 1662.

A prayer for the seven gifts of the Holy Spirit

Lord Jesus, give me the Spirit of Wisdom,
to set my heart on things that are above,
not on things that are earthly only:
give me the Spirit of Understanding,
to illuminate my life with your divine truth;
give me the Spirit of Counsel, to help me find the right words
at the right time for the right people;
give me the Spirit of Inward Strength,
to bear my cross for your sake,
and overcome with courage all that obstructs my following in
    your Way:
give me the Spirit of Knowledge,
to behold the Holy Trinity – one God –
and know myself, even just a little;
give me the Spirit of True Godliness,
to find your service sweet and joyful, and its own reward;
give me the Spirit of the Fear of the Lord,
to fill me with reverence and wonder at your will and works.
In your name I make this prayer. Amen.

Traditional prayer, adapted

Questions

1 Should it matter whether we think of God in terms of Father, Son and Holy Spirit?
2 How do you encounter the Holy Spirit in daily life?
3 Is it true that 'love is all you need'?
4 Do we need to use words to make sense of God?
5 Have you ever felt that you were not worthy of the love of God?

4

Falling asleep

────•◦•────

Acts 7.54–60, RSV

Now when they heard these things they were enraged, and they ground their teeth against him [Stephen]. But he, full of the Holy Spirit, gazed into heaven and saw the glory of God, and Jesus standing at the right hand of God; and he said, 'Behold, I see the heavens opened, and the Son of man standing at the right hand of God.' But they cried out with a loud voice and stopped their ears and rushed together upon him.

Then they cast him out of the city and stoned him; and the witnesses laid down their garments at the feet of a young man named Saul. And as they were stoning Stephen, he prayed, 'Lord Jesus, receive my spirit.' And he knelt down and cried with a loud voice, 'Lord, do not hold this sin against them.' And when he had said this, he fell asleep.

2 Corinthians 4.3–12, RSV

Even if our gospel is veiled, it is veiled only to those who are perishing. In their case the god of this world has blinded the minds of the unbelievers, to keep them from seeing the light of the gospel of the glory of Christ, who is the likeness of God. For what we preach is not ourselves, but Jesus Christ as Lord, with ourselves as your servants for Jesus' sake. For it is the God who said, 'Let light shine out of darkness,' who has shone in our hearts to give the light of the knowledge of the glory of God in the face of Christ. But we have this treasure in earthen vessels, to show that the transcendent power belongs to God and not to us. We are afflicted in every way, but not crushed; perplexed, but not driven to despair; persecuted, but not forsaken; struck down, but not destroyed; always carrying in the body the death of Jesus, so that the life of Jesus may also be manifested in our bodies. For while we live we are always being given up to death for Jesus' sake, so that the life of Jesus may be manifested in our mortal flesh. So death is at work in us, but life in you.

When I was training for the priesthood at theological college, we were given guidance and teaching about how to handle death, and in particular how to help others through bereavement, with all the issues it might raise for them. Part of this teaching included a firm instruction that we ought never to use euphemisms for death. It was not helpful, we were told, to talk about someone being 'passed on' or having 'gone over' or 'departed'. They had not 'fallen asleep' or 'left the room'. They were dead. So we must talk about 'the dead person' and his or her 'death'. There was much pastoral wisdom in this, for it forced us as future clergy to avoid the trap of being mealy-mouthed and instead to speak realistically about a subject which is very much taboo in polite circles. Death is death, and no amount of euphemistic speech can make it otherwise. God knows it is hard enough to accept that we shall never see the dead again in this life; so a little plain speaking would mainly be a good thing, provided it were done sensitively and gently. At a time of bereavement, when even the simplest words seem charged with powerful meaning and lasting significance, and especially when everyone else is trying their hardest to use any form of words but the 'D'-word, it can be a relief to hear someone speaking, at last, the simple factual truth.

The irony is, as you may have noticed if you have just read through Acts 7.54–60, that the Bible *does* use some apparently euphemistic terms for death. On occasions it does seem to be sidestepping the bluntness of the word itself. It is probably more accurate, however, to call these terms 'metaphors' or 'images' – for the word 'euphemism' suggests an attempt to disguise something essentially distasteful, which in terms of the Christian attitude to death will turn out to be far from the case. Here Stephen, the first Christian martyr, is stoned, and as a result, the text says, 'he fell asleep'. What might this cryptic phrase mean? We have to consider whether it is only a euphemism – a way of disguising the harsh reality of death – or whether it is an honest expression of what dying as a Christian ought to be like. Stephen's death was a violent one, yet Scripture speaks of it as if it were a tranquil and peaceful conclusion. This falling-asleep in death sets the pattern for all future Christian dying, whether traumatic or untroubled. We find exactly the same wording in the story of a hermit of the fourth century called Pambo, who lived in Egypt, weaving baskets and dispensing wisdom to all who came to see him: 'Shortly after this time the man of God *fell asleep*, not because of fever or disease but as he was making a little basket, in the seventieth year of his age.'[1]

The writer who recorded this little story clearly saw it as a beautiful death, not a way of sidestepping the physical realities of the event, even though he describes details which must bring them vividly to mind – such as the act of wrapping the body in linen and carrying it to the grave. This seems to suggest that to describe Christian dying as 'falling asleep' implies not annihilation or extermination, but rather entering a different state, a new realm and way of being, where the parameters are utterly different – yet we are still who we always were. To find out whether this is correct, we can now go on to see what the Gospels have to say on the subject.

If we turn to the most significant death in the Bible, that of Jesus himself, we find that it too is described in oblique terms rather than with a wholly straightforward statement. I have used here, in each case, the translations which most closely follow the original Greek:

Jesus cried again with a loud voice and yielded up his spirit.

(Matthew 27.50, RSV)

Jesus gave a loud cry and breathed his last.   (Mark 15.37, NRSV)

Jesus, crying with a loud voice, said, 'Father, into your hands I commend my spirit.' Having said this, he breathed his last.

(Luke 23.46, NRSV)

Jesus said, 'It is finished' and he bowed his head and gave up his spirit.   (John 19.30, RSV)

There are significant variations among the four evangelists on the precise terminology, but more importantly there is a powerful overall consensus – Jesus spoke out loud and breathed his last, or yielded up his spirit. The words for 'spirit' and breathe' are very

---

[1] The story of Pambo the hermit is recorded by Palladius of Helenopolis (AD c.363–c.430: *Lausiac History*, 10). This is my translation from the Greek text edited by G.J.M. Bartelink, *Palladio. La storia Lausiaca* (Verona: Fondazione Lorenzo Valla, 1974).

closely connected, so that we could perhaps get closest to the original Gospel idea by saying 'he breathed his last breath' or 'he stopped breathing'.

At the very moment itself, all four evangelists choose not to use the usual, straightforward noun and verb for death and dying when they describe the actual moment of the death of Jesus. Many Bible translations are less sensitive than the original Greek they are trying to express, and turn the poetic into the prosaic by saying bluntly that 'Jesus died'. This is an unhelpful rejection of the careful phrasing of the original – but a lot depends on whether you think the Gospel writers meant exactly what they said, or whether they were using general phrases for death which would have been current at the time. For my part, I am sure that they chose their precise words with great care to make it clear to readers that dying was something Jesus himself *did*, rather than having it happen to him or be inflicted upon him. Many clergy, and those with medical or other relevant experience, will know examples of people who do seem to be able to choose the moment when they let go of life. They can manage to wait until an important date has passed, or until a loved one has arrived at their bedside; they wait until a relative has left (sometimes after the person has been with them for many hours) so that they can be alone at the moment of letting go. An elderly lady called Grace, whom I used to visit both at home and in hospital, sounded very clear about when she would be ready to go, telling her niece, who was visiting her in her last illness, not to bring some clean night clothes for the next day, 'You needn't bother,' she said, 'because I shan't be here.'

Leaving aside this intriguing observation about the possibility of our choosing the moment of our own death, there is no suggestion whatever that the Gospel writers were unclear about the *fact* that Jesus had actually died. John, for example, goes on moments later to remark that the soldiers who went to break Jesus' legs found that 'he was already dead' (this time using the routine term, John 19.33, rsv). But the evangelists apparently had their own ideas about the right way to express what happened, and it looks to me as if they chose their words with care. What we really need to take on board and make sense of is the fact that, in all four Gospels, dying is something which Jesus himself actively *does*, it is not something which he passively *endures* or which is done *to* him.

This is surprising, for we do not usually think of death as something we *do*, but as something which happens *to* us. When we take this together with the death of Stephen, the scriptural way of talking of death is even more distinctive – for although we use 'falling asleep' as a metaphor for death, we would not normally use it for violent deaths such as the one inflicted upon Stephen. It is common enough in English churchyards to see headstones with the inscription 'fell asleep in Jesus' – and it is even more common in Wales to see the equivalent expression, *a hunodd yn yr Iesu*. If this is not euphemistic, in other words if it really expresses what Christians who have buried loved ones think about the meaning of death, then we have to take that view seriously, even if it raises difficult questions about whether harsh reality is being (in our eyes) avoided. It starts to look as if Christian dying may be more complicated than we thought; and even that dying could be something Christians need to find a way to welcome and embrace, not to fear.

In the traditional way of praying the glorious mysteries, this section of the prayer focuses on the death of Mary the mother of Jesus. It either follows the tradition that she was bodily assumed into heaven (like Elijah; 2 Kings 2.11) or the view that she mystically 'fell asleep' and was afterwards transported to heaven as one resurrected, redeemed and glorified. This is because for many centuries Christians thought of Mary as the first person to live a redeemed life, based on faith in Jesus, and in true and full discipleship. So she came to be seen as a kind of pioneer in the mysterious journey towards salvation in Christ. Taken on its own, outside the context of the development of this belief, this emphasis on Mary can seem like a step too far, based on very little solid evidence. It may feel unhelpful to focus so completely on a single human being. So why has that tradition arisen, and why has it persisted among many (though not all) Christian peoples? I suggest it is a natural extension of human curiosity and anxiety about death, combined with a thorough and intelligent combing of the Scriptures for clues to the unknown future. If we want to find out what it means to die *in Christ* it makes a lot of sense to look at the first person to live a redeemed life: and that means turning to Mary because she was the first to respond to the news of the Incarnation with faith and obedience. Underneath all the centuries-thick layers of sentimental piety and theological bickering there is here a nugget of pure fact.

For now, the first thing to say about the business of dying is what Jesus says about it – namely, that it is something of which God always takes notice:

> Do not fear those who kill the body but cannot kill the soul; rather fear him who can destroy both soul and body in hell [Gehenna]. Are not two sparrows sold for a penny? Yet not one of them will fall to the ground apart from your Father. And even the hairs of your head are all counted. So do not be afraid; you are of more value than many sparrows. (Matthew 10.28–31, NRSV)

God is there with us in the process of dying, according to Jesus' own words. Perhaps that ought to be all that needs saying, for (apart from taxes) death is the only inescapable certainty in life. This inevitability, taken together with the unshakeable conviction of life continuing after death which the resurrection evoked in people, led to a reasonable and logical conclusion: Christians quickly came to see earthly life as a training, a preparation for falling asleep in death. What is earthy, earthly and fleshly cannot last for ever; but what is spiritual and redeemed is eternal (1 Corinthians 15.48–49). By the time the first letter of Peter was written, the task of Christian living was firmly established as a battle between the lower and higher aspects of the human person: 'Dearly beloved, I beseech you as strangers and pilgrims, abstain from fleshly lusts, which war against the soul' (1 Peter 2.11, AV).

All this effort and struggle is motivated by the way they understood death as a gateway to life: believing that we fall asleep to this life, only to wake up in the new and better life of the world to come, where God 'will wipe every tear from their eyes. Death will be no more; mourning and crying and pain will be no more, for the first things have passed away' (Revelation 21.4, NRSV).

That vision of heaven as our eternal home is something worth striving for, just as, in life, Jesus' vision of the kingdom of heaven is worth working to bring about on earth. The sheer glory of the vision of heavenly eternity dazzles our minds; we know full well it is beyond our imagining. When Jeremy Taylor wrote his visionary poem 'Of Heaven' which ends the introduction to this book (p. xvii), he lavished attention on the details in a spirit of wonderment, but one which was still firmly grounded in Scripture: all those details were drawn from biblical descriptions of what heaven will be like.

One pair of phrases from that poem, though, sounds an echo within the text which comes not from Scripture but from Jeremy Taylor's personal intuition about what heaven will be like, and from his insight into the faith. He imagines heaven as both an 'eternal pleasure' and an 'eternal clarity'; these are details not of external appearance but of *our own interior reactions* – the being of God is for us an eternal clarity; while the presence of God himself is an eternal pleasure. By the time we reach this stage of exploration, we have long since left behind the realms of fact and theory, word and argument: here all that matters is vision and understanding, as we realize that we are coming home. It is a promise of complete openness and full knowledge: 'Now I know only in part; then I will know fully, even as I have been fully known' (1 Corinthians 13.12, NRSV).

Our everyday environment, whether in town or countryside, is crammed with reminders of this hope that one day we shall both know and be known; and that death will not be the end of us. The very first sentence of Greek I read for myself was on a memorial tablet outside the chapel in St John's College, Oxford, and it said, once I had learned enough Greek to decipher it, 'I am the resurrection and the life': the words on that memorial stone, and millions of other memorials like it, are a ringing rejection of the counsel of despair which insists that this life is all there is. Our church buildings, churchyards and cemeteries are covered with monuments, gravestones, windows and paintings which proclaim this extraordinary Christian belief – even the word 'cemetery' itself derives from the Greek for 'falling asleep'!

As with the churches and the war memorials, we are so accustomed to these multiple proclamations that we have become desensitized, and consequently forgetful. It takes the eyes of children, or those new to church, to see with fresh vision how our Christian surroundings declare to us the truths of our own faith, and the real meaning of Christian dying. In my experience, children who visit churches are always quick to notice the skulls which decorate tombs, or which sit beneath the cross on representations of Calvary to remind people of the old belief that Jesus was crucified on the same spot where Adam had been buried. They have not learned to be polite or inhibited about death, and so are openly very interested in it. We may try in vain to fix their interest on the symbolism of font, pulpit and altar, when they find death (and animals, such as eagle lecterns) so much more attractive and interesting.

We adults, of course, are just as interested in death as children, but with two major differences. We are much more aware than most children (though not all) that the deaths of people long ago are a spur to thinking of our own death; and we are more aware than virtually all children that the business of dying is really the last stop in a long journey of physical deterioration from the unselfconscious energy and strength of youth. Often what people think of as a fear of death is really much more an anxiety about this process of ageing, fuelled, of course, by a society which values youth and tries to keep the ageing process out of the public eye as if it were something indecent – 'ageing is the new nudity', as you might say.

To add to these anxieties there is also the inexpressible mysteriousness of death and dying. Jesus draws our attention to the uncertainty, the apparent arbitrariness, of God's choosing who gets death, and who life, when he talks about there being two men in the field – 'one is taken and one is left' – or 'Two women will be grinding at the mill; one is taken and one is left' (Matthew 24.40–41, RSV). So we ask ourselves, is the act of choosing between the one and the other random? Can we influence whether we are the one taken or the one left, can we ensure by our actions that we end up in the right group? How can we even know which group is the right one? The possibility of divine judgement being exercised between one person and another opens up a new field for us to worry about – I shall say more about this in the next chapter. It is enough for now to notice that choices of all kinds are particularly fraught with anxiety for us, because *we run the risk of choosing wrongly*. If we have no choice, we have no responsibility for what happens to us; but when we are faced with a choice between one option and another, we become, through that act of choosing, responsible – which in some cases could mean blameworthy. We cannot help knowing that there is no fairness about the way we are born; some are born rich, secure and loved, others into poverty, violence and neglect. Money does not buy happiness, but it can buy security. It cannot buy health, but it can buy a better chance. There is no reason to suppose, then, that our dying should be fair either. Like being born, it will happen to all of us, and we shall have limited choice, or no choice, about the how or the when.

Even when we have a choice about the long stretch of existence between our being born and our dying, we are not free from anxiety. Every choice we make about how to live our lives will have consequences, for which we, whatever our background and upbringing, shall have to be responsible, and perhaps accountable. Should we choose to live an honest life? Who should we make friends with? What career ought we to follow? Which subjects should we study? Where should we live? Which is the right church to attend? What kind of God are we giving our love and loyalty to? And when we have no choice, and are therefore not responsible, when we are on the receiving end of other people's choices, we are not yet free from fear: who can forget the helpless grimness of being the last to be picked for a sports team at school?

With more than one Christian church claiming to be the only true Church of God, and insisting that no one can be saved unless they belong to it, it is not unreasonable for individual Christians to be concerned about where the truth is to be found, and about the importance of preparing yourself for divine judgement. For centuries Christianity has taught that heaven is for the believer, and hell for the unbeliever. It is a conviction which has been the cause of much grief and pain, indicating not only a final, total separation perhaps from those who matter very much to us, but also everlasting pain and punishment for those destined for that unbelievers' hell. This was certainly a source of pressing concern in times gone by – in front of the priest's stall in the parish of Gamlingay where I was rector, there was a monument on which someone decided to record a stern warning about death on the tomb of their loved one: 'You, O reader, be always ready: for you know neither the day nor the hour!' Such monuments form a dialogue between the living and the dead – as if messages are being passed between one world and another. Of course, we know that cannot really be so – the story of the poor man Lazarus in the Gospel is very clear on the point that there is a great gulf fixed between these two realms, and none may cross it. This grim belief in final separation into the saved and the damned has always been the majority view in Christianity. But there is another interpretation of the facts, less dominant but (to my mind) more legitimate, more realistic and more consonant with the gospel message. There will be more to say on this in the next chapter.

I am not qualified to speak with authority about how the physical process of dying works. Nor am I qualified by experience to tell readers how it feels. I can, however, reflect on the business of managing dying from a family and pastoral point of view. I mentioned earlier that clergy tend to forget how death and dying burst cataclysmically into people's lives in the most disruptive way – our job is to render it more bearable, more manageable, more normal; to use familiar things such as music, prayer and actions to get people through the unfamiliar wilderness of a world from which someone important in their life is suddenly missing. Along with those in similar professions, we spend a lot of time talking to the terminally ill, and to the bereaved. If we are lucky, this helps us to accept the naturalness of death, even when the process or moment of dying has been terribly traumatic. Yet the truth is that every profession involved with dying, whether emergency services, medical staff, funeral services or clergy, each deals with only a little piece of the picture. Even the dying person has but a partial vision of the process. So part of the answer to learning to live with dying is recognizing how we experience its impact only from our own perspective. I think this is true even when our love for others is involved as part of the bereavement process – such as helping a brother or sister come to terms with the death of their child. We can sympathize, but we cannot become them, or experience it from their unique point of view. Jesus alone came to be the focal point at which all human experience of death intersects with God's love – at the centre of the cross.

There was a time when most babies were born at home, without expert medical assistance. There was also a time when most people died at home, without intrusive medical intervention. It is popular to lament the medicalization of both 'natural' processes, as if doctors and nurses were the enemies of a happy outcome. As far as birth is concerned, this is also something of a political issue – there are definite factions supporting the right of women for a home delivery, or for pain relief on demand. The aim of both sides is to minimize risk to baby and mother; it is only the means to achieving that end which is in dispute. When it comes to dying, we have been slower to emphasize the importance of people being able to choose between home, hospice and hospital as the right place to die. The days when funerals took place only a day or two after a death, and when the body of the dead person was laid out by the women of the family and kept at home until the burial, have almost entirely gone. So even when a death happens at home, we rush to insulate ourselves from the trauma of keeping close company with the recently dead. There is no right or wrong in all this, but there are consequences; and seeing the mortal body of someone we knew, once it is bereft of the breath of life, is like looking at an uninhabited house – it does not look at all like someone who has just 'fallen asleep'.

For this reason, among others, I think we should not be too quick to discard that biblical metaphor of 'falling asleep' as a way of talking about death. It does not necessarily mean that we are deluding ourselves that the person will reawaken at any moment, or that he or she is not really dead. It is speaking much more positively than negatively, thinking about the pleasantness of falling asleep rather than (as we might otherwise see it) the dreadfulness of dying. At the moment when we come to fall asleep, we are often at a time of day when we have returned from the public world of personae and pretension – we have unwound, spent time with loved ones, lost ourselves for a little while in the imagined worlds of other people through television or a book, said our prayers, and, if we are lucky, we then slip into unconsciousness. We are still completely who we were when we were awake; but we are in a different state of being, in which time is meaningless and all the ordinary rules of physical existence are suspended. It is not such a bad image for death after all. When that last 'falling asleep' comes to us in death, when 'the busy world is hushed, the fever of life is over and our work is done' (BCP 1928), that 'work' to which this much-loved prayer refers is no longer our daily labour, but the whole work of our earthly life. Here is a challenge to live that whole life in sure and certain hope; in the knowledge of God's love but also of our duty to 'use aright the time that is left to us'.

The message we read in the physical nature of our earthly lives is one of disintegration – in other words, a message of decay, decline and breaking apart. Firmly set against this physical disintegration is the gospel message of wholeness and re-formation, which is what 'integration' really means (an integer, in mathematics, is a *whole* number). God's word builds up what human nature can only take apart, or see (or cause to) disintegrate. The pattern of living we learn from God is one that builds up, that creates, and makes, and re-forms.

In every action of this kind we are imitating God our Maker. To call God a Creator is to describe more than just his actions in history: it is also a witness to the instinct he has implanted in every one of us – to strive for wholeness and integration, to build and to plant (Jeremiah 1.10). Death seems to be a denial of this. On a macrocosmic scale, it breaks up relationships, tears families apart and punches holes in the fabric of society. On a microcosmic level, it means the disappearance of the physical being of someone we know, someone who matters to us – someone whose body is broken down into ash, or reunited with the ground from which, in that unforgettable phrase from Scripture, we were made and to which we must return (Genesis 3.19).

Christianity teaches that God not only notices that we exist, but also knows us fully and completely, and loves us as his own children. No wonder that our dying is, in his sight, no matter of indifference. This life is not a test (what if we fail?) or a punishment (what did we do wrong?); it is a *gift*; for God declares that everything he has made is more than 'good', it is '*very* good' (Genesis 1.31) – and we are included in that. The model of family is a helpful way of understanding our relationship with God; perhaps our earthly life is like a spiritual adolescence, a time of trauma and changing understanding, shifting perspective. All the biblical images for human life on earth turn out to be true together – a journey, a battle, an education, a contest, an ascent. It is not surprising that some biblical images for death will turn out to contain truth as well; if we are blessed, death will be a farewell for a little while; a falling asleep; a raising up; a planting, growth, blossom and fruiting; a harvest; a gathering together of the flock, the household, the family.

A prayer for falling asleep

Lord Jesus, you are the Way,
as well as the destination of my journey:
help me to overcome whatever stands
between the fact of your goodness
and the weakness of my faith,
so that when at last I fall asleep in you
I may see fulfilled your promise
of love and light and life eternal.
In your name I make this prayer. Amen.

Questions

1 Do we find it difficult to talk openly, and frankly, about death?
2 Should we take notice of the exact words the Bible uses to describe death?
3 How much notice do you take of the symbols of death we encounter in daily life (in memorials, churchyards, etc.)?
4 Are dying and death interesting?
5 Is home the best place to be when the time comes to die?

5

Crowning

---

1 Peter 5.1–11, RSV

So I exhort the elders among you, as a fellow elder and a witness of the sufferings of Christ as well as a partaker in the glory that is to be revealed. Tend the flock of God that is your charge, not by constraint but willingly, not for shameful gain but eagerly, not as domineering over those in your charge but being examples to the flock. And when the chief Shepherd is manifested you will obtain the unfading crown of glory. Likewise you that are younger be subject to the elders. Clothe yourselves, all of you, with humility toward one another, for 'God opposes the proud, but gives grace to the humble'. Humble yourselves therefore under the mighty hand of God, that in due time he may exalt you. Cast all your anxieties on him, for he cares about you. Be sober, be watchful. Your adversary the devil prowls around like a roaring lion, seeking some one to devour. Resist him, firm in your faith, knowing that the same experience of suffering is required of your brotherhood throughout the world. And after you have suffered a little while, the God of all grace, who has called you to his eternal glory in Christ, will himself restore, establish, and strengthen you. To him be the dominion for ever and ever. Amen.

1 Corinthians 15.51–58, RSV

Lo! I tell you a mystery. We shall not all sleep, but we shall all be changed, in a moment, in the twinkling of an eye, at the last trumpet. For the trumpet will sound, and the dead will be raised imperishable, and we shall be changed. For this perishable nature must put on the imperishable, and this mortal nature must put on immortality. When the perishable puts on the imperishable, and the mortal puts on immortality, then shall come to pass the saying that is written: 'Death is swallowed up in victory.' 'O death, where is thy victory? O death, where is thy sting?' The sting of death is sin, and the power of sin is the law. But thanks be to God, who gives us the victory through our Lord Jesus Christ. Therefore, my beloved brethren, be steadfast, immovable, always abounding in the work of the Lord, knowing that in the Lord your labour is not in vain.

At last we have reached the end of this extraordinary prayer. The glorious mysteries take us from the utter darkness of the tomb to the place of unimaginable glory 'where there shall be no darkness nor dazzling but one equal light'. Those familiar words were once preached by John Donne (Sermon 15, at Whitehall in 1627), and he ended his sermon with a prayer which expresses, purely and simply, the Christian hope – 'Keep us, Lord, so awake in the duties of our callings, that we may thus sleep in thy peace, and wake in thy glory.' This movement from darkness to light is also a movement from ignorance to knowledge, from lack of understanding to spiritual enlightenment. We have journeyed from a place of impenetrable mystery and isolation (the tomb) to the place (heaven) where the secrets of all hearts are revealed, and all things have been disclosed, and where, at last, we shall know fully, even as also we are known (1 John 3.20; Psalm 44.21; 1 Corinthians 13.12).

At both extremes the prayer invites us to enter imaginatively into a world we have never experienced, but of which we are always aware, at the edge of our consciousness. On the one hand there is death, with its final disintegration of the physical self. On the other hand there is the eternal life of the heavenly realm. There are people who describe visionary states of being which take them a little closer into these mysteries – through near-death or out-of-body experiences. The Bible occasionally records such experiences of visionary and mystical encounter (Job 4.12–21; Acts 10.9–16; 2 Corinthians 12.1–4; Revelation 4). These are an interesting but controversial subject, and although the phenomenon of near-death and out-of-body experiences is recorded across many cultures and periods of history, it is not something in which we all share by virtue of our common humanity. When it comes to interpreting what the Scriptures have to say about that other realm, though, there is a wealth of information available for every reader to receive, from the fragmentary glimpse to the full poetic vision with which the Bible closes.

I mentioned earlier in this book that Christian history has a *shape*: that Christians have believed, and in the past have felt certain, that God's relationship with the world is *providential*. This is a way of expressing our conviction that life is not meaningless – it has both purpose and direction. We have a task in hand, over the course of our earthly life, of preparing ourselves for eternal life. What is more, we have a part to play in God's plan of salvation. This sense of direction is reflected in the scope and shape of the Scriptures themselves. That arrangement of the individual books is not random. The fact that a Hebrew Bible (our Old Testament) has a completely different arrangement tells us immediately that the Christian way of putting the books together has a meaning. The Hebrew Bible begins in the same order as the Christian Old Testament, but after the first five books (known as the Pentateuch, or the Torah, the books of the Law) and the history books Joshua–II Kings, the Hebrew Bible puts the prophets together as a group (except for Daniel, they are in the same order as the Christians' Bible). Last comes the category known as the Writings, which includes Job, Psalms, Proverbs and Daniel. So the Hebrew arrangement of the books is thematic; but the Christian arrangement is *historical*: starting with the Pentateuch and history books it fits all the writings together in a chronological sequence culminating in the prophets. This shows the unfolding of God's purposes in historical time.

The Christian Bible begins with the world's beginning, as Creation is formed out of nothing by our Creator God. Its Old Testament ends with a prophetic foreshadowing of the end time:

> Behold, I will send you Elijah the prophet before the great and terrible day of the LORD comes. And he will turn the hearts of fathers to their children and the hearts of children to their fathers, lest I come and smite the land with a curse. (Malachi 4.5–6, RSV)

The New Testament does a similar thing when it ends with the vision of heavenly glory which is God's promise for all who love him, and with a prayer which every Christian should use: 'Amen. Come, Lord Jesus! The grace of the Lord Jesus be with all the saints. Amen' (Revelation 22.20–21, RSV).

We are promised heaven for all who believe. But for many people, the notion of believing in a reality we cannot see is so alien that there is simply nothing to be said, no common ground from which to engage in discussion with those who do believe in heaven. This book is not the place to take on that enormous topic; but I do have to acknowledge here the fact that such doubts about heaven are common to non-believers and some believers alike. And no wonder. Science may be a specialism for the very few at its highest level, but almost all of us have absorbed a simple version of its principles which makes believing in what cannot be seen extremely difficult.

How is it, then, that I (and I am not alone in this) can still find not only the concept of heaven but also the reality of it so easy to believe in? I have no answer to this. I only know that I do believe, and that the fact of my believing is something gifted to me from outside my own self (rather than something I have imagined or invented). The same is true of my belief in divine providence. I do not think that factual argument is much more help to us here than it is to those who want to argue about the existence or non-existence of God. Factual argument can undermine our confidence, disturb our peace or build us up in knowledge and understanding; but it cannot stop the instinct to believe, because that instinct is inherent in us. It is born in us and, if we give it the right environment to flourish, it will grow in us too.

Let us pause now for a moment and consider some problems which the idea of an end time and a final judgement bring forth. Not everyone in the world is a Christian. Nor do most of us believe that it could ever be possible (never mind appropriate or right) to convert everyone in the world. Not all Christians believe the same things about God, and since their beliefs are often contradictory, not all Christians can always be right about God. Not all who say they are Christian behave in a Christian way, or live what they say they believe.

Where do these factual negatives point us as we begin to think about life after this life? Is eternal life for the chosen few, the true believers, the elect? Or is it for everybody? Each of us begins with the potential to be formed and shaped by God. Each of us ends – where? Surely Christian teaching over the centuries has set two possibilities before us, not one. Surely there is not only heaven, there is hell as well!

The concept of heaven can be a stumbling block to belief because we can't see where or what it is, how it exists apart from this world or interpenetrates it; and because we can't understand what heavenly existence is like – even the words of Jesus only give us the briefest of clues. If heaven can be a stumbling block because we can't understand it, hell is a worse one. There was a time when hell was one of the Church's most powerful weapons, perhaps even its unique selling point. The fear of divine judgement and the terrible possibility of eternal torment brought many into subjection to the power of the Church. But it was bad for them, and bad for the Church too. If you have ever stood looking at a painting of the Last Judgement, you will know how fascinating such pictures can be: full of gloating cruelties in the details of individuals discovering, at this moment of judgement, that their eternal destiny is to be pain and torture. All those malicious demons, and the torments beyond belief. No wonder people were once worried enough to do what the Church told them. No wonder there was perpetual anxiety about whether they had done enough to satisfy God's demands.

What possibilities were there for that 'final destination'? First, from the days of the Old Testament, there was *Sheol*,[1] which we looked at briefly in Chapter 2, 'Ascension' (see p. 24). There the dead coexist in a shady half-life which seems to make no separation of the righteous and the sinners. Then there is *Hades*,[2] a New Testament word taken over from pagan Greek literature. Like Sheol it usually refers to the world of shades, and of the insubstantial, undifferentiated dead. Another New Testament word for the world of the dead is *Gehenna*.[3] This one is a specifically Jewish word for a place where human sacrifice and burning had taken place in history, and which had thus become a place of abomination. Jesus often used the term 'Gehenna' to describe God's rejection of evil; and he spoke of it as a place of destruction, where the fire would be unquenchable. This is usually the word behind the English translation 'hell'.

Thus the concept of a shady abode of the dead combined with that of a judgement after death. Two ideas emerged: one emphasized belief in a place of transition (Hades), the other belief in a final place of punishment (Gehenna). Different Bibles translate these terms in different ways, sometimes in ways which obscure these distinctions

---

[1] Pronounced 'sh-ohl' (stressing the second syllable) to rhyme with 'toll'.
[2] Which rhymes with 'ladies'.
[3] Which rhymes with 'Mackenna'.

so that it is often difficult to see which idea is really being referred to. Even when we are clear about the precise terms, there is still room for debate about whether the righteous go straight to heaven (Luke 23.43) or whether they wait in Hades until the end time and the day of resurrection (Revelation 14). Various early Christian writers put forward their ideas about how hell worked and who went there, based on a combination of Scripture and reason. In the third century, one of the great theologians of the east, Origen, applied his considerable intelligence and ingenuity to the problem. Origen knew his Bible down to the smallest detail, in Hebrew and in Greek. But his deep knowledge did not drive him into fundamentalism. On the contrary, it liberated his interpretation of the Bible. Armed with his knowledge of Scripture and his understanding of the nature of God, Origen concluded that an endless punishment of sinners in the unquenchable fires of hell was unworthy of a God who, because he was a God of love, must use discipline only for remedial purposes, not for vengeance. If a soul were made by God to suffer in hell, that could only be in order to effect a restoration, a cure. Once the soul was cleansed, it ascended to heaven, just as Christ had done. What God had brought about, therefore, by the Incarnation, resurrection and atonement wrought in Jesus Christ was the restoration of all humankind to that state which God had always intended for them.[4]

More than a century later another great theologian, Gregory of Nyssa, returned to this idea (which had now come to look slightly dodgy because of disputes over Origen's orthodoxy). Gregory also argued that the punishment of souls in hell must be not vindictive but restorative, to return the soul to the state God originally intended for it. Gregory understood evil itself as the absence of good, so he also thought that when every will is freely turned to God there will be no more evil, and Paul's words will be fulfilled – 'God may be all in all' (1 Corinthians 15.28, AV). So a day will come, Gregory insisted, when every intelligent being will be restored to friendship with God. And he meant *every* intelligent being:

> Over long periods of time, once the evil of our nature is removed
> (which for now is mixed in with our nature and grows up as part of

---

[4] The word Origen used was *apocatastasis*, which means 'a restoration to an original state' (originally of a planet in orbit coming full circle).

it) when the restoration [the Greek word is *apocatastasis*] to an original state of those presently stuck in wrongdoing takes place; all creation will unite in harmonious thanksgiving – both those who were disciplined for their purification and those who never needed purification . . . Christ freed humankind from evil and healed even the inventor of evil himself [Satan].[5]

That was daring when he wrote it – it is still a shocking thought today. The idea of hell as entirely restorative, as nothing to do with retribution, ought to astound and shock us. It is so completely different from what the Church has taught for many centuries. In the Western tradition, in which most of us are rooted, the standard view is that Satan's wickedness is eternal. This is based on texts from Scripture: 'He himself [Christ] likewise partook of the same nature, that through death he might destroy him who has the power of death, that is, the devil' (Hebrews 2.14, RSV).

Perhaps the most familiar example of this teaching is the great battle:

Now war arose in heaven, Michael and his angels fighting against the dragon; and the dragon and his angels fought, but they were defeated and there was no longer any place for them in heaven. And the great dragon was thrown down, that ancient serpent, who is called the Devil and Satan.   (Revelation 12.7–9, RSV)

One standard mainstream reference work on Christianity, *The Catholic Encyclopedia*,[6] confidently states that: 'The Holy Bible is quite explicit in teaching the eternity of the pains of hell. The torments of the damned shall last for ever and ever.'

As if that answered our questions about fairness; and the relationship between our nationality and place of birth, our upbringing and education; about how well we were taught the faith; about whether abuse or cruelty from within the institution of the Church made trust (never mind faith) impossible for us! What about people who live and die without the chance to encounter Christian faith? What will God do with them? And with the people who lived and died before Christianity was born? We are not in a position to

---

[5] Gregory of Nyssa, *Catechetical Oration*, 26 (my translation).
[6] *The Catholic Encyclopedia* (New York: Robert Appleton, 1908–12).

be dogmatic about this. It is possible, even reasonable, to argue from such Scriptures that the Bible clearly insists on the reality of the tormenting flames of hell. It may be, though the matter is much less clear and precise than some would have us believe, that it is possible, by our actions and choices, to put ourselves perpetually beyond the reach of God's love – in other words, that the torments of the damned in hell are everlasting. The greatest theologian of the Western tradition, Augustine, accepted the argument that God condemns sinners to eternal punishment. Yet Augustine thought that hell was not a place but a state of being, of separateness from God, which in itself is a form of torment. In time, the subtlety of his vision gave way to something simpler, more satisfyingly retributive and vengeful: that the baptized are saved, and that the unbaptized are damned, and damned for ever, to hell, a place of unquenchable fire and endless torment.

All his life Augustine wrote to explain and defend the faith which he loved and in which he had been saved. He couldn't find a way round the idea of the eternal torment of the damned in hell, because of the way he read his Bible. He felt unable to accept the idea that ultimately all are saved. Yet the overarching principle of every one of his many writings was that love stands at the centre of all things: that God is love, and that our capacity for love is God-given. Augustine insisted that any interpretation of the Bible which does not accord with, or result in, the love of God or the love of our neighbour cannot be correct. And that is where I too take my stand. I must acknowledge the fact of Bible passages which talk of hell, and its fiery punishments for sinners. I must acknowledge the fact that many intelligent, distinguished and spiritual Christians have believed in hell and damnation and eternal torment. But I must also insist that it is possible to think otherwise, and to do so with full Christian integrity. It is possible to find in Scripture the truth that hell may be eternal, and its fires may be eternal, because the human capacity for wrongdoing is never-ending. But there is no necessity for any Christian to believe that those who end up in hell are condemned there for eternity. Jesus often refers to hell (Gehenna), but never says that those who are sent there are left there *for ever*. The root of the word 'damnation' points us to the idea of suffering a *loss*. Hell, as I understand it, and as I think the Bible describes it, is about *losing God*. We experience the sense of losing touch with God repeatedly in our lives. But the possibility of losing God for ever is something which, I think, I hope, God's eternal forgiveness and boundless love will not allow. It is for this reason that the most compelling interpretation of hell that I have ever read comes from a children's story by C.S. Lewis. In *The Last Battle*, the scene which is most painful (because it is the scene which paints our capacity for self-torment in the clearest colours) is that which unfolds after a number of the characters, both human and non-human, find themselves transported to heaven. For some, the glory of our eternal home is in plain sight; but for others (in this case some of the dwarfs) the glory is invisible, and the pleasures which for the rest are in plain view, and within easy reach, cannot be tasted and enjoyed because they have not the heart, or mind, or soul, to apprehend them. Thus Lewis gives us a perfect depiction of how we can create our own hells in this world or the next.

So the problem with hell, theologically, is not the use of the image of fire to stand for cleansing and purification; this is familiar from the Old Testament ('he is like a refiner's fire'; Malachi 3.2, RSV). Unless we think we are already perfect in this life, how can we *not* need to be purified, to prepare us for the glories that are to be revealed? What is more, we know that every pain we endure, every moment of suffering we encounter, has the power to change us not for worse but – if we choose so, if we can endure it – for better. This is *not* the same as saying that God makes us suffer in order to punish us or to correct us. The theological problem with hell only comes if we think of the pain endured there as inflicted for eternity. That is monstrous even by human standards; and by the standards of divine compassion it is an abomination.

With this final mystery, we have reached the end of the traditional prayers of the rosary. We have journeyed from the first moment of the Incarnation ('Annunciation' in my earlier book *Joyful Christianity*) all the way through the sufferings of Jesus' passion up to the crucifixion (in *Passionate Christianity*) to the ultimate restoration of all human-kind in accordance with God's love and his providential care, here at the end of the glorious mysteries. The worst of our nature was revealed in the moment when Jesus was wounded and mocked with the weav-ing of a crown of thorns, set upon his head to hurt and humiliate him ('The crowning with thorns' in *Passionate Christianity*). That act of cruelty has been healed and transformed in the final mystery of the traditional prayer: in exchange for the crown of thorns which we set upon our Saviour's head, he has given us crowns of gold as signs that we are fellow-heirs with him of the kingdom of God. So a promise made to a king of Israel long ago in song has become a blessing to us for the future which we now know is not the end but rather the beginning of life in all its fullness: 'You meet him with rich blessings; you set a crown of fine gold on his head. He asked you for life; you gave it to him – length of days forever and ever' (Psalm 21.3–4, NRSV).

Every single one of these ancient prayers has taught us to focus on Jesus and his true identity, his real significance – as we meditate on each one, we are meant to discover more about Christ dwelling in us. In this final mystery of the crowning, the moment when we attain our ultimate goal of the heavenly city, the new Jerusalem, we have finally come into our inheritance: 'Come, you that are blessed by my Father, inherit the kingdom prepared for you from the foundation of the world' (Matthew 25.34, NRSV).

When I pray the glorious mysteries, I find it very difficult to meditate upon this vision of glory, not because I don't believe in it, but because its wonder and beauty are so far beyond the capacity of my poor imagination. This is nothing to do with a deficit of suggestions. The Scriptures are full of visions of the glory that is to come. The book of Revelation describes that glory in dazzling detail, which Jeremy Taylor reflects in his poem. Heaven is the place where we can lay our burdens down, and be clothed in white and crowned with gold, and sing praises, and find at last our abiding home in our Father's house. There are probably many people who pray this mystery and meditate on the vision of heaven, without difficulty, but I am not one of them. Instead I find myself drawn back to this present world, and as I pray, I picture the faces of people I love, or know, or work with; and I pray for them, offering them to God for healing and for blessing. Sometimes I begin the glorious mysteries knowing that there are people I want to pray for; and so the initial mysteries become a preparation for that final one in which I hold particular people before God in prayer for his help and healing. At other times faces float into my mind unbidden and unexpected, but I do not fight the inclination, I just follow where the Spirit guides me and pray for whoever comes to mind. There is no right or wrong in how we pray the mysteries, but that is my way.

In the traditional understanding of this final mystery, as with that in the previous chapter, meditation usually focuses on Mary the mother of Jesus, as the first to know the truth of the Incarnation and the first to be redeemed by Jesus through her obedience to God's will as revealed in Christ. But the real point is that Mary stands for all of us who are redeemed, and that helps me to hold to God in prayer the people who matter to me, and to rejoice in their salvation, as, at the same time, I give thanks for my own.

I think of the theology I have been exploring and explaining here as the foundation on which such prayer is built. We need to do the spadework and prepare the ground for prayer; and theology is one of the main materials with which we build. But once the groundwork is completed, we can start to construct the building itself; and then the foundations are hidden from view and superseded in thought. Precisely because we have done that theological groundwork properly, we do not need to keep on worrying about it, but to get on with other things.

In these glorious mysteries, as in all the mysteries, we have found our own lives inextricably bound to the life of Jesus. We have also found ourselves re-made in his image, as his brothers and sisters, his fellow-heirs. We have discovered our faith to be mysterious and complex, but also reasonable and full of hope. There is nothing left to do after all this but to follow the call and to walk in the way. At last we can do so confident that the prophetic name of Jesus – Emmanuel – given to him centuries before the Incarnation, has at last been revealed to us, and in us. He truly is God-with-us. And we shall be his people, and he will be our God.

A prayer for our crowning

Lord Jesus, I thank you that your love
sets no limit to faith, hope or endurance:
you have promised that where you are,
one day I shall be there also;
so grant me courage to step out daily without fear
into the unknown future –
my hand in your hand,
my heart in your keeping,
day by day.
In your name I make this prayer. Amen.

Questions

1 Do you think near-death experiences have anything to teach us about the life of the world to come?
2 Is it helpful to see the Bible as historical, or a revelation of God's providence?
3 Do heaven and hell exist?
4 Shall we meet any non-Christians in heaven, if/when we get there?
5 Do you feel that you have a sense of what heaven will be like?

Final word

The way to judge of Religion is by doing of our duty,
and Theology is rather a Divine life than a Divine knowledge.
In Heaven indeed we shall first see, and then love;
but here on earth we must first love,
and love will open our eyes as well as our hearts,
and we shall then see and perceive and understand.

Jeremy Taylor, *Via Intelligentiae*, 1662, p. 13